Seven Principles of

# RATIONAL EMOTIVE
# BEHAVIOUR THERAPY

# Seven Principles of

# RATIONAL EMOTIVE
# BEHAVIOUR THERAPY

**Windy Dryden**, PhD

Rationality Publications

Rationality Publications
136 Montagu Mansions, London W1U 6LQ

www.rationalitypublications.com
info@rationalitypublications.com

First edition published by Rationality Publications
Copyright (c) 2021 Windy Dryden

A catalogue record of this book is
available from the British Library.

First edition 2021

ISBN: 978-1-910301-91-3

# Contents

# Introduction

This is the second book in the 'Seven Principles' series, where I discuss seven fundamental principles that explain the essence of a particular therapeutic topic. This book outlines the seven key principles of Rational Emotive Behaviour Therapy (REBT) as I see them.

In *Principle 1*, I discuss the concept of emotional responsibility whereby a client takes responsibility for their emotions by recognising that these feelings are underpinned by a set of attitudes which they hold. Given that the client holds these attitudes, they can be said to be responsible for them and thus responsible for their emotions. As I make clear in this principle, the client needs to assume emotional responsibility without blaming themself. Having made the point that attitudes are crucial to taking emotional responsibility, I outline the four main attitudes that underpin a client's emotionally disturbed responses to actual or inferred adversities and the four main attitudes that underpin a client's emotionally healthy responses to the same adversities.

Following on from making the point that attitudes are vital in understanding healthy and unhealthy responses to adversities, in *Principle 2*, I discuss the value of the client *feeling bad* in the face of adversities and how this should be a goal of REBT. While this initially sounds a strange idea to clients – and you, dear reader, may also find it strange yourself at first reading – once I have explained this point then it will be clear what I mean and why the REB therapist wants to help the client to feel (healthily) bad when facing an adversity.

All effective therapists are mindful of the importance of developing and maintaining a good working alliance with their clients. In *Principle 3,* I outline REBT's position on what constitutes a good working alliance in this approach to psychotherapy. In doing so, I describe the four components of the alliance: bonds, views, goals and tasks – and show how the REB therapist strives to develop and sustain a good working relationship with the client in each of these four components.

Careful assessment of both a client's problems and problem-related goals is crucial to effective REBT practice. In *Principle 4,* I outline my 'Situational ABC' assessment framework and discuss several techniques that I have created to make this assessment process as accurate and efficient as possible. Without a careful assessment of a client's problems and goals, the effective practice of REBT would be significantly compromised.

Facilitating change is, of course, the heart of any therapeutic approach. In *Principle 5,* I focus my discussion on how the REB therapist promotes attitude change in their client. While most of this principle is devoted to furthering attitude change, I also discuss other forms of change – inferential change, frame change, behavioural change and environmental change. This shows that REBT is not a 'one-trick' pony and advocates a flexible position in fostering whatever change the client is open to and capable of.

REBT is an approach to therapy that offers the client many concepts, ideas and practices which are unique to REBT and engender doubts, reservations and objections (DROs) in the client. In *Principle 6,* I discuss the most common of these DROs and outline how the REB therapist can help the client identify a particular DRO, formulate it, and examine it until it is no longer a DRO.

In *Principle 7,* I end the book by discussing the different levels of help a client may seek from the REB therapist. In particular, I distinguish between issues of disturbance, dissatisfaction and development that the client might bring to therapy and make a case that these issues should ideally be addressed in the order outlined. However, again REBT is flexible, so if a client wants to work with a different order, the therapist will accommodate their wishes and preserve the working alliance between them unless the therapist has a good reason not to do so.

At the end of the book, I present a brief further reading list for those who want to study REBT in greater depth. I hope you find this book of value and I would appreciate any feedback that you may wish to give me sent to windy@windydryden.com.

*Windy Dryden*
*February 2021*

# PRINCIPLE 1

# Encouraging Emotional Responsibility: For Attitude Is Key

One of the critical tasks that the REB therapist has at the beginning of therapy is to encourage the client to see what they are responsible for and what they are not responsible for. Thus, the client is responsible for what is in their control – their behaviour, feelings, and attitudes they choose to take towards life events. They are not responsible for what is not in their control – others' behaviour, others' emotions, and the attitudes that others take towards life events. They can influence other people, but others are responsible for how they respond to these influence attempts.

In this chapter, I will concentrate on the importance of encouraging clients to assume emotional responsibility and to maintain this throughout the therapeutic process and beyond. Emotional responsibility means that the client acknowledges and even embraces the idea that they are primarily responsible for the way they feel through the attitudes that they hold towards the events in their lives.

This is more difficult than it sounds, particularly when the client is facing highly aversive life events. Consequently, it needs to be done with a great deal of sensitivity; otherwise, it will interfere with the working alliance that the therapist seeks to develop with the client (see *Principle 3*). REBT theory is helpful here because it distinguishes between negative emotions that are healthy and negative emotions that are unhealthy. This means that the therapist can help the client see that they will inevitably experience a negative emotion when facing an adversity. This will be the case unless they try to convince themself that what matters to them does not matter to them. For if the client faces an adversity, it is healthy for them to feel bad about it. However, they have a choice between whether that negative emotion is healthy or unhealthy. I will discuss this more fully in *Principle 2*.

## The Key Role of Attitude[1]

Perhaps the most central aspect of REBT theory concerns the role that attitude plays in determining whether a person's emotional response to an adversity is negative and healthy or negative and unhealthy. REBT argues that healthy negative emotional reactions to adversities are based on four critical attitudes, and unhealthy negative emotional responses to the same adversities are based on four very different equally vital attitudes. The REB therapist helps the client understand what these attitudes are and see that they can choose to hold one set of attitudes over the other. Since the client is responsible for the choice of attitudes that they hold, as argued above, they can be said to be responsible for their emotions according to the

---

[1] In this book, I use the word 'attitude' instead of 'belief' and prefer the terms 'rigid/extreme attitudes' and 'flexible/non-extreme attitudes' to the terms 'irrational beliefs' and rational beliefs'. I have explained the reasons for this change in nomenclature in Dryden (2016).

attitudes that they choose to hold. I will now review these two sets of four attitudes.

## Rigid Attitudes vs Flexible Attitudes

REBT acknowledges that a client is likely to have desires that indicate what is important to them and what they want to happen and what they wish not to happen. The therapist encourages the client to acknowledge their desires and not to change them. Their desires per se, then, are not centrally implicated in the client's emotional problems. Thus, if a client wants to be respected, for example, and they are not respected, their desire for respect is not problematic. REBT theory argues that a person has a choice of keeping a preference flexible or making it rigid. Thus, the client can hold a flexible attitude towards respect (e.g. 'I want to be respected, but I don't have to be respected') or a rigid attitude towards respect (e.g. 'I want to be respected and therefore I have to be respected').

If we look at this a little more closely, we find that both attitudes have a *preference component*. I refer to this as a 'shared component'. When the person makes their desire rigid, they add an *asserted demand component*. I refer to this as a 'distinguishing component' in that it distinguishes between a rigid attitude and a flexible attitude. It characterises the former, not the latter.

'I want to be respected (preference component) and therefore I have to be respected' (asserted demand component)

However, when they keep their desire flexible, they add a *negated demand component*. This is also a 'distinguishing component' that distinguishes between a rigid attitude and a flexible attitude. It characterises the latter, not the former.

'I want to be respected (preference component), but I don't have to be respected' (negated demand component)

In the face of adversity (i.e. not being respected), if the person holds a flexible attitude, as shown above, they will experience a healthy negative emotion (HNE). If they hold a rigid attitude, as shown above, they will experience an unhealthy negative emotion (UNE). As they can choose whether to hold a flexible or rigid attitude and are responsible for that choice, they are responsible for that choice's emotional consequences.

Figure 1.1 summarises the points discussed in this section.

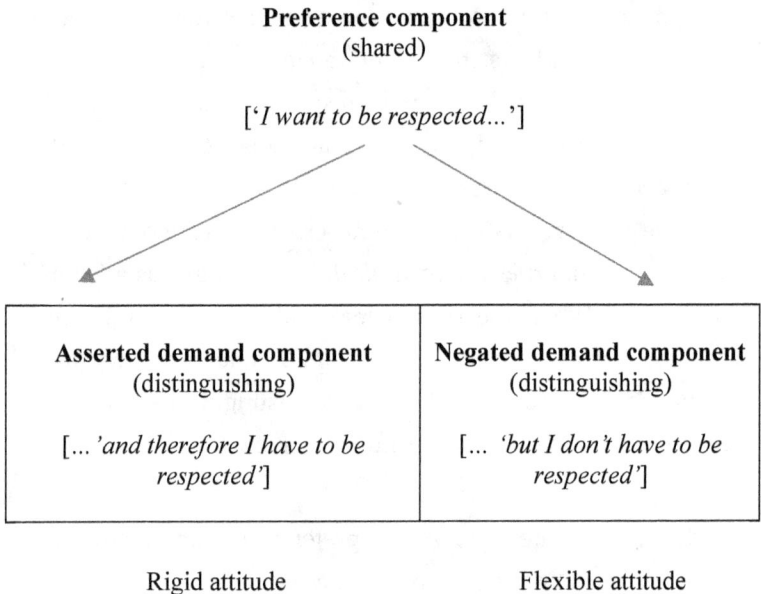

**Preference component**
(shared)

['*I want to be respected...*']

| **Asserted demand component**<br>(distinguishing)<br><br>[... '*and therefore I have to be respected*'] | **Negated demand component**<br>(distinguishing)<br><br>[... '*but I don't have to be respected*'] |
|---|---|

Rigid attitude                    Flexible attitude

**Figure 1.1**    The Components of Rigid and Flexible Attitudes

## Extreme Attitudes vs Non-Extreme Attitudes

Albert Ellis, the REBT founder, argued that of the four attitudes underpinning a client's emotionally disturbed response (UNE) towards an adversity, a rigid attitude is at the core of this response. He also argued that three extreme attitudes – an awfulising attitude, a discomfort intolerance attitude and a devaluation attitude – are derived from this rigid attitude. Additionally, Ellis argued that of the four attitudes that underpin a client's emotionally healthy response (HNE) towards an adversity, a flexible attitude is at the very core of that response. He further argued that three non-extreme attitudes – a non-awfulising attitude, a discomfort tolerance attitude and an unconditional acceptance attitude – are derived from this flexible attitude. I will now compare each extreme attitude with its non-extreme attitude counterpart.

### *Awfulising Attitudes and Non-Awfulising Attitudes*

When a person does not have their desires met, this is neither a cause for celebration nor indifference. Instead, it is expected that the person would make an evaluation that it is bad when their preference is not met. However, they have a choice whether to make this evaluation extreme or keep it non-extreme. When the person makes their evaluation of badness extreme, they take their non-extreme evaluation and convert 'it is bad' into 'it is awful/horrible/terrible' (e.g. 'it is bad not to be respected, and therefore it would be awful if this happened'). On the other hand, when the person keeps their evaluation of badness non-extreme, they begin with 'it is bad', but negate the extreme evaluations listed above (e.g. 'it is bad not to be respected, but it isn't awful').

Thus, an awfulising attitude comprises an *evaluation of badness component,* which is the 'shared component' and an *asserted awfulising component* which is a 'distinguishing component' of the awfulising attitude. In contrast, a non-awfulising attitude comprises the same shared *evaluation of badness component* and a *negated awfulising component* which is the 'distinguishing component' of the non-awfulising attitude.

Figure 1.2 summarises the points discussed in this section.

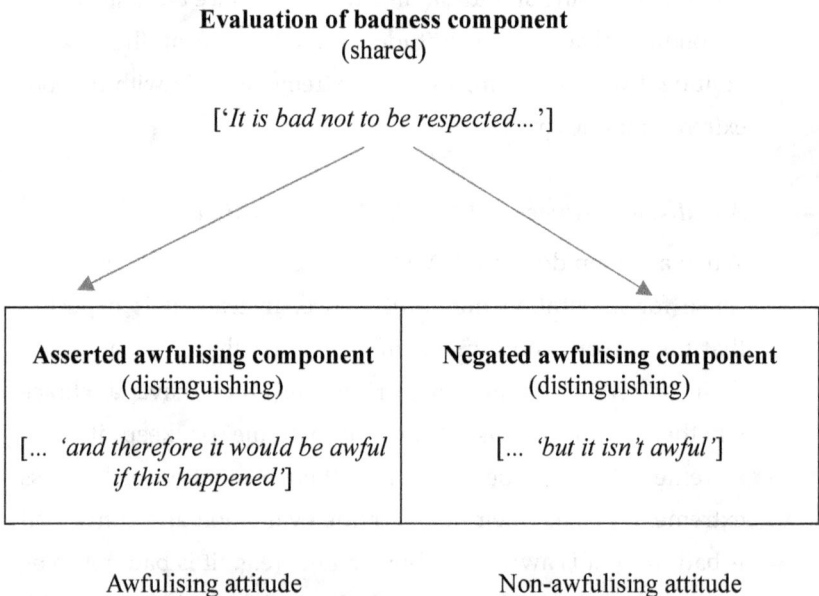

**Evaluation of badness component**
(shared)

['*It is bad not to be respected...*']

| **Asserted awfulising component** (distinguishing) | **Negated awfulising component** (distinguishing) |
|---|---|
| [... '*and therefore it would be awful if this happened*'] | [... '*but it isn't awful*'] |

Awfulising attitude                    Non-awfulising attitude

**Figure 1.2** The Components of Awfulising and Non-Awfulising Attitudes

## *Discomfort Intolerance Attitudes and Discomfort Tolerance Attitudes*

When a person does not get their desires met, whatever attitude they bring to this adversity, they will struggle to deal with it. However, their choice is to bring an attitude of discomfort intolerance or an attitude of discomfort tolerance to this struggle.

When the person brings an attitude of discomfort intolerance to the struggle, they are adopting an extreme position concerning the struggle (e.g. 'It is a struggle for me to tolerate not being respected and therefore I couldn't bear it'). However, when the person brings an attitude of discomfort tolerance to the struggle, then they are adopting a non-extreme position to the struggle (e.g. 'It is a struggle for me to tolerate not being respected, but I could bear it. It is worth it to me to bear it, I am willing to do so and I am going to do so').

An attitude of discomfort intolerance has two components, a *struggle component,* which is 'the shared component' and a *discomfort intolerance component,* which is the 'distinguishing component' of the discomfort intolerance attitude. On the other hand, a discomfort tolerance attitude comprises five components, the same shared *struggle component* as in the attitude of discomfort intolerance, a *discomfort tolerance component,* a *worth tolerating component*; a *willingness to tolerate it component* and a *going to tolerate it component.* The latter four components are 'distinguishing components' of the discomfort tolerance attitude.

Figure 1.3 summarises the points discussed in this section.

**Struggle component**
(shared)

[*'It is a struggle for me to tolerate not being respected...'*]

| Discomfort intolerance component (distinguishing) | Discomfort tolerance component **Worth tolerating component** **Willingness to tolerate it component** **Going to tolerate it component** (distinguishing) |
|---|---|
| [... *'and therefore I couldn't bear it '*] | [... *'but I could bear it. It is worth it to me to bear it, I am willing to do so and I am going to do so '*] |

Discomfort intolerance attitude          Discomfort tolerance attitude

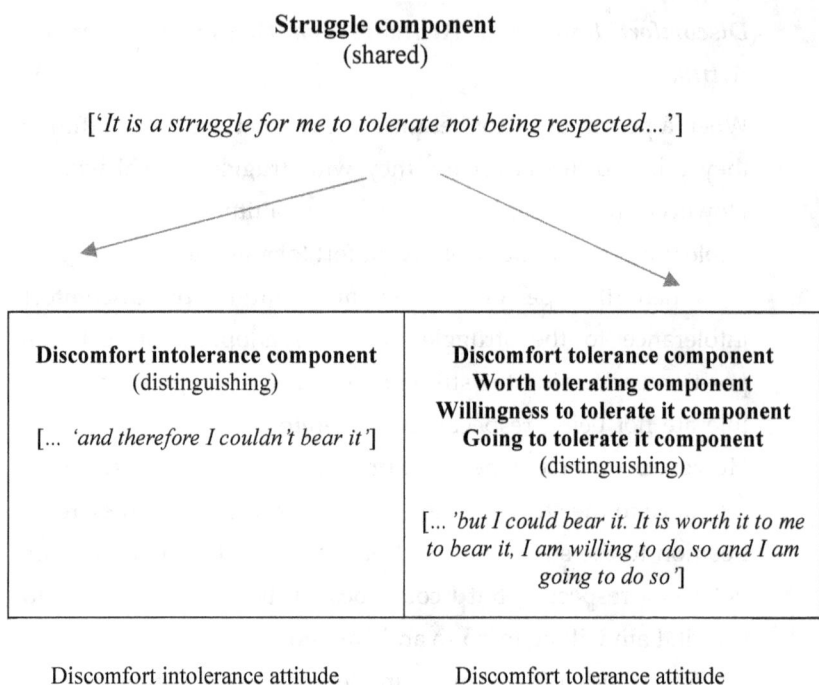

**Figure 1.3** The Components of Discomfort Intolerance and Discomfort Tolerance Attitudes

### Devaluation Attitudes and Unconditional Acceptance Attitudes

When a client does something negative or has a negative experience, they will negatively evaluate this aspect. I call this a *negatively evaluated aspect component*. This is a 'shared component' as it is common to both devaluation and unconditional acceptance attitudes. As before, the client has a choice concerning which of these two attitudes to hold. There are three different devaluation attitudes and three different unconditional acceptance attitudes. When the client holds themself responsible for their negative behaviour or negative experience, they will either devalue or accept themself. If they hold another person responsible, then they will adopt either a devaluation or unconditional attitude towards that person. Finally, if they hold life responsible, they will either adopt a devaluation or unconditional acceptance attitude towards life.

A devaluation attitude has two components, a *negatively evaluated aspect component*, which is the 'shared component', and a *global devaluation component* (e.g. 'It is bad that I was not respected and this proves that I am unworthy'). This is the 'distinguishing component' of the devaluation attitude.

By contrast, an unconditional acceptance attitude has three components: a *negatively evaluated aspect component*, a *negated global devaluation component* and an *asserted fallibility/complexity component* (e.g. 'It is bad that I was not respected but it does not prove I am unworthy. I am a fallible, complex human being whether I am respected or not'.) The last two components are 'distinguishing components' of the unconditional acceptance attitude.

Figure 1.4 summarises the points discussed in this section.

**Negatively evaluated aspect component**
(shared)

[*'It is bad that I was not respected...'*]

| **Global devaluation component** (distinguishing) [... *'and this proves that I am unworthy'*] | **Negated global devaluation component Asserted fallibility/complexity component** (distinguishing) [... *'but it does not prove I am unworthy. I am a fallible, complex human being whether I am respected or not'*] |
|---|---|

Devaluation attitude                    Unconditional acceptance attitude

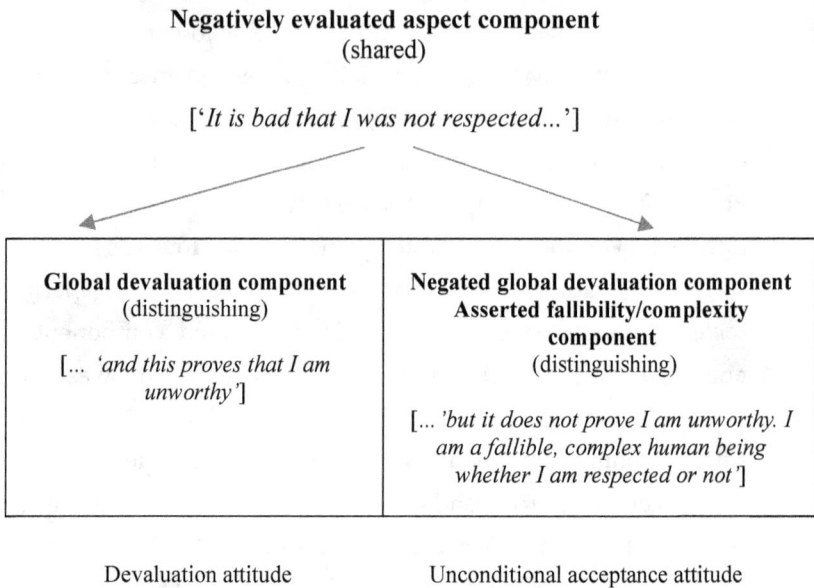

**Figure 1.4** The Components of Devaluation and Unconditional Acceptance Attitudes

*

In the next principle, I will discuss an important distinction made in REBT between unhealthy negative emotions and healthy negative emotions. I will explain why the REB therapist encourages the client to set the latter as a goal with respect to facing an adversity.

# PRINCIPLE 2

# Promoting the Value of Feeling Bad (But Not Disturbed) in the Face of Adversity

In *Principle 1*, I outlined REBT's principle of emotional responsibility and discussed the differences between holding a set of rigid and extreme attitudes, on the one hand, and holding a set of flexible and non-extreme attitudes, on the other. As I will show in *Principle 4*, the REB therapist uses an 'ABC' framework to help themself and their client understand the factors involved in the client's emotional problem and what they need to change to solve this problem. In the framework, 'A' stands for the adversity that features in the client's problem, 'B' stands for the basic attitudes that underpin the client's disturbed responses (at 'C' – the consequences) to this adversity and those that underpin their possible healthy responses (also at 'C') to the same adversity. As I detailed in *Principle 1*, the basic attitudes that underpin the client's disturbed responses to 'A' are rigid and extreme, and those that underpin their healthy responses to 'A' are flexible and non-extreme.

## What Are Healthy Responses to an Adversity?

After a client has nominated a problem to discuss in therapy and has explained the problem to the REB therapist, the latter will ask the client what they see as a healthy way of handling the situation

21

that they currently find problematic. Such a question often takes the client off guard because they generally have never considered it. They have a problem, and their goal is not to have the problem, pure and simple. However, if the question is considered in greater detail with the client, then they will see that the answer is not as simple as they previously thought.

As shown above, an adversity at 'A' features in the client's problem and the REB therapist needs to help the client to see that the best way of addressing the adversity with a view to changing it, is for the client first to respond to it in an emotionally healthy way. The client will often think that this involves them not experiencing their unhealthy negative emotional reaction (UNE) to the adversity at all (e.g. 'I don't want to be anxious') or to experience it with lesser intensity (e.g. 'I want to feel less anxious'). The first client remark above is problematic because a client cannot *not* respond emotionally to an adversity. They need to respond in some manner. The second client remark is also contentious for if an unhealthy negative response such as anxiety is problematic, having a less intense version of it is still problematic.

### What Is an Emotionally Healthy Response to an Adversity?

REBT theory argues that as the client deems an adversity to be negative, they can be expected to experience a negative emotional response to this adversity. Therefore, it is not healthy for the person to feel nothing in response to the adversity as they would have to hold the following attitude towards the adversity to achieve this ('It does not matter to me that the adversity has occurred'). This is an indifferent attitude, and it is based on falsehood as it does matter to the person that the adversity has occurred. If it truly did not matter, the person would not experience a problem since the adversity would not be seen as an adversity! An adversity is so named because its presence or absence matters to the client.

It is also not healthy for the person to have a positive emotional response to the adversity. To achieve this, they would have to hold the following attitude towards the adversity ('It is good that the adversity occurred'). This positive attitude towards an adversity is also based on falsehood, for it is highly unrealistic for the person to be pleased that something negative has occurred in their life.

Suppose it is unrealistic for the person to feel indifferent or positive towards an adversity. In that case, the only remaining option is for the client to feel bad about the adversity's existence. Now REBT distinguishes between two different types of 'bad' feelings. Emotions that are negative in feeling tone and unconstructive in effect – these are known as 'unhealthy negative emotions' (UNEs) – and emotions that are also negative in feeling tone, but constructive in effect – these are known as 'healthy negative emotions' (HNEs). As already discussed, UNEs stem from the client holding a rigid/extreme attitude towards an adversity. HNEs stem from the client holding an alternative rigid/extreme attitude towards the same adversity.

When a client has a disturbed emotional response to an adversity, they are experiencing a UNE. When they have a healthy emotional response to the same adversity, they are experiencing an HNE. The REB therapist needs to help the client understand that they should strive in the first instance to feel healthily bad (rather than unhealthily bad) in the face of the adversity. This response is both realistic and constructive. It reflects the reality that a client will feel bad about a bad event, and it will help the person face the adversity and process it healthily.

### What Is a Constructive Behavioural Response to an Adversity?

So far, I have discussed a client's unhealthy and healthy emotional responses (at 'C') to an adversity at 'B'. When the person experiences an unhealthy negative emotion about an adversity, they tend to act in dysfunctional or unconstructive ways. If acted on, these behavioural tendencies lead the person to avoid facing the adversity or act towards it in ways that make matters worse for the person. However, when the client experiences a healthy negative emotion about the same adversity, they tend to act in functional or constructive ways. When acted upon the person will face the adversity and act towards it in ways that make matters better for the person.

### What is a Constructive Thinking Response to an Adversity?

Similarly, when the client experiences an unhealthy negative emotion about an adversity, they tend to think in highly distorted ways, skewed to the negative and ruminative in nature. If the client engages with such thinking, they will deepen their disturbance. However, when the client experiences a healthy negative emotion about the same adversity, they tend to think in realistic, balanced, and non-ruminative ways.

*Helping Clients to Understand the Integrated Nature of HNEs, Constructive Behaviour, and Realistic, Balanced, and Non-Ruminative Thinking at 'C'*

In helping the client understand the importance of working towards experiencing a healthy negative emotion towards an adversity rather than an unhealthy negative emotion, the REB therapist draws upon the ideas expressed above when the person experiences a healthy negative emotion. They will also tend to act constructively and think in realistic, balanced, and non-ruminative ways. If the client is not convinced, the therapist asks them to compare the totality of their UNE/ unconstructive behaviour/dysfunctional thinking response at 'C' with the totality of their HNE/constructive behaviour/ functional thinking response at 'C'. This usually helps the client to see that that they need to move away from the former integrated 'C' response and towards the latter.

## Different Negative Emotions (Both Unhealthy and Healthy) Reflect the Presence of Different Adversities

For me, one of the most important, but neglected concepts in the general field of CBT is Beck's (1976) concept of the 'personal domain'. A client's personal domain consists of many tangible and intangible elements deemed important by the person. The more critical the aspect, the more central it features in that person's personal domain. The nature of a person's emotional response (whether healthy or unhealthy) will depend on how the person infers the relationship between an event and their personal domain. From an REBT perspective, whether that person's emotion will be a UNE or an HNE will depend not on the inference alone but on the nature of the person's attitude towards that inference. Thus, if a person perceives a threat to their personal domain (inferred adversity at 'A'), they will experience anxiety (at 'C') if they hold a rigid/extreme attitude (at 'B') towards that adversity. However, if they make the same inference of threat (at 'A') and they hold a flexible/non-extreme attitude (at 'B'), then they will experience concern (at 'C').

This tells the REB therapist that certain inferences are associated with certain UNEs/HNEs. In my view, the therapist needs to have this information at their fingertips when working with clients. It also tells the REB therapist that inferences on their own do not tell us whether a client's emotion will be a UNE or an HNE. The therapist needs to know the client's attitude to determine that.

Table 2.1 shows the major inference-related adversities associated with each significant emotional pairing (i.e. UNE and HNE).

**Table 2.1**    Adversities with Associated Unhealthy and Healthy
Negative Emotions

| Adversity | Negative emotions | |
|---|---|---|
| | **Unhealthy** | **Healthy** |
| • Threat | Anxiety | Concern |
| • Loss<br>• Failure<br>• Undeserved plight (experienced by self or others) | Depression | Sadness |
| • Breaking your moral code<br>• Failing to abide by your moral code<br>• Hurting someone | Guilt | Remorse |
| • Falling very short of your ideal in a social context<br>• Others judging you negatively | Shame | Disappointment |
| • The other is less invested in your relationship than you<br>• Someone betrays you or lets you down and you think you do not deserve such treatment | Hurt | Sorrow |
| • You or another transgresses a personal rule<br>• Another disrespects you<br>• Frustration | Unhealthy anger | Unhealthy anger |
| • Someone poses a threat to a valued relationship<br>• You experience uncertainty related to this threat | Unhealthy jealousy | Healthy jealousy |
| • Others have what you value and lack | Unhealthy envy | Healthy envy |

## Putting Everything Together

In this principle, I have discussed the following ideas:

- REBT distinguishes between unhealthy negative emotions and healthy negative emotions.
- Unhealthy negative emotions are associated with unconstructive behaviour and highly distorted thinking that is skewed to the negative and ruminative in nature. These dysfunctional responses (at 'C') stem from rigid and extreme attitudes (at 'B') that the client holds towards adversities (at 'A').
- Healthy negative emotions are associated with constructive behaviour and realistic and balanced thinking that is non-ruminative in nature. These functional responses (at 'C') stem from flexible and non-extreme attitudes (at 'B') that the client holds towards adversities (at 'A').
- Different adversities at 'A' are linked with unhealthy and healthy negative emotional pairs at 'C'.

Table 2.2 presents a summary of these ideas.

**Table 2.2**    An Overview to Help the REB Therapist Make the Point that Healthy Negative Emotions Are Healthy Responses to Adversities

| **Adversity**<br>(in relation to the client's personal domain) | |
|---|---|
| Basic attitudes ('B')<br>(rigid and extreme) | Basic attitudes ('B')<br>(flexible and non-extreme) |
| Consequences ('C')<br>(unhealthy and unconstructive)<br><br>*Emotional* = Unhealthy negative<br><br>*Behavioural* = Unconstructive<br><br>*Thinking* = Highly distorted, skewed to the negative and ruminative in nature | Consequences ('C')<br>(healthy and constructive)<br><br>*Emotional* = Healthy negative<br><br>*Behavioural* = Constructive<br><br>*Thinking* = Realistic, balanced and non-ruminative in nature |

\*

In *Principle 3*, I discuss the point that the effective practice of REBT needs to be based on a solid working alliance between the therapist and client. In doing so, I outline REBT's stance on each of the four components of the alliance.

# PRINCIPLE 3

# Developing and Maintaining a Good Working Alliance: It Matters

While the REB therapist has in mind several strategies when working with a client and uses many techniques in the service of these strategies, it is important to remember that the implementation of these strategies and techniques occurs within the context of a relationship between the therapist and the client.

I have argued elsewhere (Dryden, 2021a) that the best way of thinking about the therapeutic relationship in REBT is to use the concept of the working alliance that was developed by Ed Bordin (1979). Bordin argued that there are three components of the therapeutic working alliance: (1) the bond, (2) goals and (3) tasks. I later added a fourth component, which I termed 'views' (Dryden, 2011). While I will discuss each component separately here, in reality, they are interdependent. For example, when the therapist and client have a shared 'view' of the main factors that explain the client's nominated problem[2] and agree with the client's goal concerning this problem, then doing so strengthens the 'bond' between them.

---

[2] I call the problem that the client has chosen to work on in a therapy session their 'nominated' problem.

## The Bond in REBT

The 'bond' component of the working alliance refers to the interpersonal connectedness between the therapist and client. There are several dimensions of this bond. I will discuss two here: REBT's position on the 'core therapeutic conditions' as initially described by Carl Rogers (1957) and the REB therapist's interpersonal style.[3]

### The 'Core Conditions'

The 'core conditions', as they have become to be known, were first introduced by Carl Rogers (1957). Applying Rogers's original thesis to a modern view of these conditions, when the client experiences the therapist to be empathic, respectful and genuine in the therapeutic encounter, therapeutic change will inevitably occur. Rogers's view that these conditions are necessary and sufficient for change to occur was challenged by Ellis (1959) who said that while these conditions may be important, they are neither necessary nor sufficient for client change to take place.

The modern term 'respect' was previously known as 'prizing', 'unconditional positive regard' or 'non-possessive warmth'. Ellis singled out this latter term as potentially problematic in the practice of REBT. Thus, Ellis (in Dryden, 1985) argued that the REB therapist needs to be cautious about being 'overly' warm towards a client in case doing so reinforces the client's dire needs for love and approval. However, this

---

[3] I refer the interested reader to Dryden (2021a) for an extended discussion of the bond component of the working alliance in REBT.

position is not generally held by REB therapists. In a study of the therapeutic core conditions in REBT and person-centred therapy, both sets of therapists were rated as being equally warm by their clients (DiGiuseppe, Leaf and Linscott, 1993).

REB theory argues that developing a good working alliance is important primarily because it helps the client be more open to the strategic and technical aspects of REBT. Whether clients share this view in REBT is not known. My stance is that the REB therapist should ideally strive to show empathic understanding of the client's concerns, demonstrate that they respect the client and be genuine in the therapeutic encounter, whether these conditions are intrinsically therapeutic or are strategically therapeutic in helping the client to be more open to the REBT way of dealing with problems. My view is that both of the above positions have therapeutic validity.

Let me now consider what REBT has to say about each of these 'core conditions.'

*Empathy*: REBT distinguishes between affective empathy and attitudinal empathy. When the REB therapist shows the client affective empathy, they convey to the client that they understand how the client feels. By contrast, when the therapist shows the client attitudinal empathy, they offer the client an REBT-based understanding that links the client's problematic feelings to the attitudes that REBT theory hypothesises underpin these feelings.

*Respect*: REB theory prefers the concept of 'unconditional acceptance' to the term 'respect'. Here, the therapist demonstrates that they accept the client as a fallible human being who is a complex mixture of good, bad and neutral features. This term differs from the concept of respect (and its synonyms, 'prizing', 'unconditional positive regard' or 'non-possessive warmth'). It does imply a positive global evaluation of the client. As shown in *Principle 1*, unconditional acceptance is an attitude based on a non-evaluative acceptance of the person while allowing for evaluations of the person's features or aspects. In sum, 'rate the parts, but not the whole'.

*Genuineness*: In REBT, the concept of genuineness is demonstrated by the therapist in three ways. First, the REB therapist does not hide behind a therapeutic facade and is pretty much the same person inside therapy as outside therapy. Second, the REB therapist is prepared to 'level' with the client and convey 'difficult to hear' messages, when therapeutically appropriate. For example, the REB therapist helps the client understand that they may contribute to others' negative behaviour towards them by the negative behaviour that they display to these others. However, the therapist takes care not to say anything that the client cannot handle. Third, the therapist demonstrates genuineness by disclosing relevant aspects of their life and how they used REBT to deal with issues similar to those discussed by the client. The therapist is mindful of showing the client that they initially struggled with the issue but dealt with the problem by using appropriate REBT methods, the same as the client may also benefit from employing. Before disclosing their personal experience, the therapist is advised to check with the client to see if they would find such therapist self-disclosure beneficial. Not all clients appreciate therapists being open about their personal experiences (Dryden, 2011).

## *Interpersonal Style*

A second aspect of the bond that is important in REBT concerns the interpersonal style that the therapist adopts in working with the client. The theoretically-driven and educative nature of REBT calls for practitioners to adopt an active-directive style in working with clients. Thus, an REB therapist is active in directing the client's attention to the rigid and extreme attitudes that underpin their problems. At least initially, the therapist takes the lead in helping the client examine and change these rigid and extreme attitudes to their flexible and non-extreme attitudinal equivalents. The client would not work attitudinally without the therapist's active and directive assistance. In adopting an active-directive style, the REB therapist needs to ensure that the client is actively engaged in the therapeutic process. The therapist needs to guard against rendering the client passive by talking too much, for example. Adopting an active-directive style in REBT is an inherent part of the therapist's interpersonal style, particularly in the early and middle phases of therapy. As the therapy process unfolds, however, and the client learns how to become their own therapist, the REB practitioner becomes less active and less directive and adopts a style where they prompt the client to use what they know and encourage them to do so.

There are other aspects of the REBT therapist's interpersonal style that need to be considered. One major one relates to the degree of formality the therapist adopts while working with the client. REBT does not take a position concerning whether the therapist should adopt a formal style of interacting with the client or a formal one. The therapist is left to determine this for themself. Clients differ concerning their preferences for interacting with their therapists with some preferring their therapist to adopt a formal and serious relational style.

In contrast, others prefer an informal, less serious style in their therapist. The effective REB therapist can vary their interpersonal style to meet the client's preference in this respect, once they have discovered it[4]. When the therapist demonstrates such stylistic flexibility and can do so with genuineness, they are being what Lazarus (1993) called an 'authentic chameleon'. That being said, I have known many REB therapists over the years, and in my experience, most REB therapists tend to favour an interpersonal style that is active-directive, informal and to some extent, humorous.

## Shared Views in REBT

Both the therapist and client have views about salient aspects of the therapeutic process. I will focus on the views that both have about the nature of the client's problems and how they can be best addressed. However, it is also important that both participants agree on such matters as confidentiality, fees and the therapist's cancellation policy.

---

[4] The easiest way the therapist can discover which style the client would find most beneficial in interacting with the therapist is for the therapist to ask the client directly at the beginning of the therapeutic process.

## The Nature of the Client's Problems

As I pointed out in *Principle 1*, the REBT view of a client's emotional problem is based on the rigid and extreme attitudes that the client holds towards the adversity that features in this problem. Therefore, it is vital that the REB therapist is explicit about this view and explain it as clearly as possible early on in the therapeutic process. Some REB therapists do this at the very beginning of therapy. Thus, Paul Woods (1991) even did this before the client discussed their problems. Albert Ellis used to teach his clients the 'Money Model' in which he explained what is known as the 'B-C' connection in REBT. This teaching device makes it clear that rigid and extreme attitudes underpin a psychologically disturbed response to adversity. In contrast, flexible and non-extreme attitudes underpin a psychologically healthy response to the same adversity (see Table 3.1).

**Table 3.1**    An Example of the 'Money Model'

*Windy:*    OK, Sarah. I'd like to teach you a model which explains the factors that account for people's emotional problems. Now this is not the only explanation in the field of therapy, but it is the one that I use in my work as an REB therapist. Are you interested in learning about this explanation?

*Sarah:*    Yes, I am.

*Windy:*    Good. Now there are four parts to this model. Here's part one. I want you to imagine that you have £10 in your pocket and that you hold the following attitude: 'I would prefer to have a minimum of £11 on me at all times, but it's not essential that I do so. It would be bad to have less than my preferred £11, but it would not be the end of the world.' Now, if you held this attitude, how would you feel about only having £10 when you want, but don't demand a minimum of £11?

*Sarah:*    I'd feel concerned.

*Windy:*    Right. Or you'd feel annoyed or disappointed. But you wouldn't kill yourself.

*Sarah:*    Certainly not.

*Windy:*    Right. Now, here's part two of the model. This time you hold a different attitude which is. 'I would prefer to have a minimum of £11 on me at all times and therefore I absolutely must have at least that amount on me at all times. I must! I must! I must! And it would be the end of the world if I had less.' Now, with this attitude you look in your pocket and again find that you only have £10. Now, how would you feel this time about having £10 when you demand that you must have a minimum of £11?

*Sarah:*    I'd feel quite panicky.

*Windy:*    That's exactly right. Now, note something really important. Faced with the same situation, different attitudes lead to different feelings. Now, the third part of the model. This time you still have the same attitude as you did in the last scenario, namely, 'I would prefer to have a minimum of £11 on me at all times and therefore I absolutely must have at least that amount on me at all times. I must! I must! I must! And it would be the end of the world if I had less.' This time, however, in checking the contents of your pocket you discover two pound coins nestling under the £10 note. How would you feel about now having £12 when you believe that you have to have a minimum of £11 at all times?

*Sarah: ....*    I'd feel very relieved.

*Table 3.1 continued*

*Windy*:      Right. Now, here is the fourth and final part of the model. With that same £12 in your pocket and that same attitude namely: of the model. This time you still have the same attitude as you did in the last scenario, namely, 'I would prefer to have a minimum of £11 on me at all times and therefore I absolutely must have at least that amount on me at all times. I must! I must! I must! And it would be the end of the world if I had less', one thing would occur to you that would lead you to be panicky again. What do you think that might be?

*Sarah*:      Let me think... My attitude is that I must have a minimum of £11 at all times, I've got more than the minimum and yet I'm anxious. Oh, I see I'm now saying 'I must have a minimum of £13.'

*Windy*:      No. You are sticking with the same attitude as before namely: 'I must have a minimum of £11 on me at all times. I NOW have £12...'

*Sarah*:      Oh! I see... I NOW have the £12. Right, so I'm scared I might lose £2.

*Windy*:      Or you might spend £2 or you might get mugged. Right. Now the point of this model is this. All humans, black or white, rich or poor, male or female make themselves disturbed when they don't get what they demand they must get. And they are also vulnerable to making themselves disturbed when they do get what they demand they must get, because they could always lose it. But when humans stick rigorously (but not rigidly) to their non-dogmatic preferences and don't change these into rigid musts then they will feel healthily concerned when they don't have what they prefer and when they recognise that their preferences don't have to be met. And when their hold this flexible attitude, they will be able to take constructive action under these conditions to attempt to prevent something undesirable happening in the future. Now in our work together we will pay close attention to the differences between rigid and flexible attitudes. Is that clear?

*Sarah*:      Yes.

*Windy*:      Well, I'm not sure I've made my point clearly enough. Can you put it into your own words...?

Most REB practitioners use the client's nominated problem to outline the REBT view of such problems. Thus, my approach is to take the client's nominated problem and assess it using the 'ABC' framework (see *Principle 2*). Here I will focus on the client's rigid and alternative flexible attitude. First, I identify the client's primary disturbed emotion at 'C'; then, I discover their adversity at A. Second, I help them see that they have a preference regarding their adversity, which is common to their rigid attitude or flexible attitude. Third, I ask them which attitude underpins their problem: the preference component plus the asserted demand component (rigid attitude) or the preference component plus the negated demand component (see *Principle 1*). They almost always select the former. Fourth, I ask them how they would feel about the adversity if they had a firm conviction in their flexible attitude. This way of working makes explicit the 'B–C' connection for the client's problem and offers a 'B–C' analysis of what could potentially be the client's goal concerning responding healthily to the adversity.

Whichever method the REB therapist uses to make explicit the REBT view of the client's problem, it is vital that the therapist elicits the clients' doubts, reservations or objections (DROs) to REBT's ABC model and deal with whatever issues the client raises. I will discuss the importance of doing this more fully in *Principle 6*. If by disclosing their DROs, the client is helped to understand the 'ABC' model better and is thus willing to use it going forward, therapeutic progress has been made. However, suppose the client has a different view. In that case, therapy can still proceed, but only if they and their therapist both arrive at a shared understanding that can prove useful to the client, which does not involve the 'B–C' connection. Otherwise, the client may be better served by a therapeutic approach that is more congruent with their views on the nature of their problems.

### How the Client's Problems Can Best Be Addressed

The REBT view of therapeutic change follows from its view of the nature of emotional problems. This means that to deal effectively with their emotional problems, the client needs to change their rigid/extreme attitudes to their flexible/non-extreme attitude alternatives. Sometimes, however, the client is unable or unwilling to change their attitudes at 'B'. In which case, the therapist can negotiate a solution to their problem based on changing their inferences at 'A', changing the 'A' altogether, changing their behaviour at 'C', or combining these non-attitudinal solutions.

## Goals

All forms of therapy are goal-directed. It is not easy to conceive a situation where a person comes to therapy without having a purpose in mind. From an alliance perspective, the vital issue is that the client and therapist agree on the client's goals and work towards achieving them. In REBT, goals can be discussed at different points of the therapeutic process.

### Session Goals

There is a viewpoint in therapy that stems from single-session therapy (SST) which states the following. As a therapist does not know for sure in the first session whether or not a client will come back for a second session, this influences the therapist's goal-setting at the very beginning of therapy. Thus, a therapist may ask a question like, 'If, when you get home this evening, and you reflect on the session, what would you have achieved to make you pleased that you came today?' This is known as the client's session goal.

### Goals Concerning Problems-as-Experienced

When a client nominates a problem to discuss with their REB therapist, and the therapist asks them what they want to achieve from discussing the issue, then it is likely that the client's goal will be quite vague. This is because they are thinking about the goal regarding their problem as they experience it. For example, imagine Carl, who told me that he has an anxiety problem when he has to speak in public when the focus is on him. If I as his therapist asked him what he wanted to achieve from seeking help for this problem, he might have said something like, 'I don't want to be anxious when I speak in public' or 'I want to be confident about speaking in public.' These goals can be seen as endpoints and as such, are not based on an assessment of the client's problem. To achieve this 'endpoint' goal, Carl needs to achieve prior goals based on an REBT-assessment of his problem (see *Principle 4*).

### Goals Concerning Problems-as-Assessed

When the client nominates a problem, they describe it based on their own experience as noted above. At this point, the REB therapist and the client need to develop a more in-depth understanding of the problem and to do this, the therapist uses REBT's ABC framework. When the therapist and client have done that, the client can be helped to set a goal underpinned by this assessment. In Carl's case, he was anxious about going blank while giving his speech. His goal was to be healthily concerned rather than anxious about this possibly happening.

### Helping the Client to Understand the Relationship between Different Types of Goals

As can be seen, goals can be considered at different phases in therapy, and it is the REB therapist's task to help the client understand the relationship among these goals. For example, the client needs to realise that they need to pursue goals related to assessment before expecting to achieve goals related to their problems as experienced. This is also the case when considering the client's disturbance-related goals and development-related goals. Mahrer (1967) argued that there are two primary psychotherapy goals: to help clients overcome their disturbance and help them develop themselves. The latter is now seen as the province of coaching, which I will discuss briefly in *Principle 7*.

## Tasks

Tasks are activities carried out by the therapist and the client directed towards the client's goal. I present the major tasks that the REB therapist and the client have to implement in Tables 3.2 and 3.3.

**Table 3.2**    The therapist's tasks in REBT

---

*The beginning phase*
- Develop a working alliance
- Collaborate with the client throughout
- Outline REBT for the client
- Begin to assess and intervene on the client's nominated problem
- Teach the ABC's of REBT
- Deal with the client's doubts, reservations and objections

*The middle phase*
- Follow through on the client's nominated problem
- Encourage the client to engage in relevant tasks
- Work on the client's other problems
- Identify and challenge the client's core rigid/extreme attitudes
- Deal with obstacles to change
- Encourage the client to maintain and enhance gains
- Undertake relapse prevention and deal with the client's vulnerability factors
- Encourage the client to become their own therapist
- Deal with the client's doubts, reservations and objections

*The ending phase*
- Decide with the client on when and how to end therapy
- Encourage the client to summarise what has been learned
- Attribute improvement to the client's efforts
- Deal with obstacles to ending
- Agree on criteria for follow-ups and for resuming therapy

---

**Table 3.3**    The client's tasks in REBT

---

- Collaborate with the therapist throughout
- Specify problems
- Be open to the therapist's REBT framework and give honest feedback
- Apply the specific principle of emotional responsibility
- Apply the principle of therapeutic responsibility
- Disclose doubts, reservations and objections
- Disclose difficulties and blocks to change

---

From an alliance perspective, the effectiveness of REBT is increased under the following conditions:

- *The client accepts the principle of emotional responsibility (see Principle 1).* Without this, the client will not engage in REBT, and thus, therapy will not be effective. A significant task of the therapist is to help the client to understand and implement this principle.
- *The client understands that they have therapeutic tasks to perform, and they know the nature of these tasks (see Table 3.3).* Again, it is the therapist's responsibility to raise this issue early in the therapeutic process.
- *The client has the ability, knowledge, and skills to carry out these tasks.* The therapist is responsible for inviting the client to consider a range of therapeutic tasks and to enquire if the client has the ability, information, and skills to implement them. However, it is ultimately the client's responsibility to tell the therapist if they do not have such ability,

knowledge, and skills.

- *The client understands the nature of the tasks they are called upon to execute and can see that performing the tasks will help them achieve their goals.* The therapist needs to keep the tasks–goals connection to the forefront of their work with the client.

- *The client accepts that they need to work to change (the principle of therapeutic responsibility – see Table 3.3) and implements this principle.* However, the therapist needs to raise this issue with the client at appropriate junctures and deal with any doubts, reservations and objections the client has to this principle (see *Principle 6*).

- *The task that the therapist asks the client to undertake has sufficient potency to facilitate the client in achieving their goal.* The therapist needs to know the research literature here and be aware that cognitive tasks on their own are often too weak to promote client change. However, cognitive tasks applied with relevant behavioural tasks have greater potency in this respect.

- *The client understands the nature of their therapist's tasks and how they relate to their own tasks and goals.* It is the therapist's tasks to help the client to come to this understanding.

- *The therapist is sufficiently skilful at implementing their tasks.* Therefore, it is important that the REB therapist has ongoing supervision and occasionally asks their supervisor to listen to and comment on recordings of their therapy sessions. An REB therapist's skills are difficult to discern from case discussion, whereas recordings of sessions allow such skills to be appraised.

As I pointed out at the beginning of this principle, the working alliance's four components are interdependent even though I have discussed them here separately.

*

In the following principle, I will discuss the importance of the therapist assessing the client's problems with accuracy and their goals in mind.

# Principle 4

# Making Assessment Adversity-Based and with Goals in Mind

A primary goal of REBT is to help the client deal effectively with the adversities in their life, whether these adversities actually happened[5] to them or the person thought that they happened. Thus, as I will discuss later, when the therapist has identified the adversity that features in the client's problem, the therapist encourages the client to assume that the adversity is real. This enables them to identify the rigid and extreme attitudes that underpin their unhealthy response to the adversity. It is also to help the client see that if they adopt alternative flexible and non-extreme attitudes towards the adversity, they would be able to deal with it healthily. In this way, assessment is both adversity-based and done with goals in mind.

---

[5] These also include adversities that are currently happening or that the person predicts will occur in the future.

## Problem Assessment or Case Formulation?

I was initially trained in REBT in the late 1970s and in Aaron Beck's approach to CBT known as 'Cognitive Therapy' (CT)[6] in the early 1980s. At the time, both approaches were problem-focused, which meant that assessing the client's problems was a vital task for the therapist. Over the years, the tradition of cognitive behaviour therapy, of which REBT and CT are featured, stressed the importance of developing a case formulation[7] with clients before treatment was initiated (e.g. Persons, 1989). This involves the therapist helping the client identify all the problems for which they are seeking help, how these problems originated, how they are related together, and the main mechanisms that account for the continued existence of these problems. A case formulation, then, is a kind of map of the client's problem-related life together with their strengths and resilience factors (Kuyken, Padesky and Dudley, 2009). This map helps both the client and therapist see the extent of their tasks in therapy and where best to begin the journey. Many CBT practitioners adopt what I call a 'formulation-based mindset' and will not start therapy without first developing a collaboratively established formulation of the client's 'case'.

---

[6] Beck and his colleagues now refer to his approach as 'Cognitive Behaviour Therapy' which is confusing as this term usually refers to the therapeutic tradition in which approaches to CBT are placed rather than any one particular approach.

[7] Some authors prefer the term 'case conceptualisation' (e.g. Kuyken, Padesky and Dudley, 2009). For our purpose here, the terms can be treated synonymously.

Interestingly, REBT therapists tend not to have this 'formulation-based mindset' when beginning therapy. They tend to have what might be termed a 'problem-based mindset' at the outset. Also, the professional training courses in REBT that are run under the Albert Ellis Institute's auspices in New York do not feature 'case formulation' as part of the training curriculum. This is not to say that the REBT therapist does not see the importance of having an overall understanding of the client's 'case', but they prefer to develop this as therapy proceeds (Dryden, 1998; DiGiuseppe, Doyle, Dryden and Backx, 2014).

REBT is problem-based for several reasons. In his practice, Albert Ellis almost always began therapy in the first session with a client. He developed this approach from his early experiences in working in a clinic where clients had to undertake several assessment sessions before therapy commenced. At first hand, Ellis saw that this 'person-based' assessment approach was inefficient in the way therapeutic time was utilised. Clients were also frustrated because, in the main, most did not want to go through an elaborate assessment procedure before beginning therapy. Instead, they wanted help with their problems at the outset. This is what they got later when Ellis started to practise what he then called 'Rational Therapy' (Ellis, 1957). Throughout his career in what was subsequently named 'Rational-Emotive Therapy' and then 'Rational Emotive Behaviour Therapy', Ellis maintained this 'therapy-based' approach to the first session. In my view, this is what makes REBT suitable to be used in what is known as 'Single-Session Therapy' (Dryden, 2019).

Most REB therapists follow Ellis's lead in ensuring that therapy is initiated in the client's first visit. This tends to mean that the client is invited to nominate a problem to discuss early on in the first session after basic information has been collected and the client has had an opportunity to tell the therapist in their way why they are seeking therapy.

When the therapist and client have agreed on a problem on which to focus (which I call here the client's 'nominated' problem), the first step is for the therapist and client to work together to develop an accurate assessment of this problem. In doing so, the REB therapist uses a framework that guides them when asking questions to elicit salient information to enable an accurate assessment to be made. This framework is known as REBT's 'ABC' framework. While all REB therapists will use this framework, different therapists have their own slightly different versions of this framework and use different language to explain it. In this principle, I will outline my version of the 'ABC' framework, and make clear which elements are commonly used and which are unique to my practice.

## The 'Situational ABC' Framework

In the version of the 'ABC' framework that I use there are four components as outlined below.

- 'Situation': A descriptive account of the context in which the problem occurred.
- 'A' = Adversity. This represents the aspect of the situation about which the client was most disturbed.

- 'B' = The basic[8] attitudes that the client held in the situation in which they experienced the problem. These attitudes are rigid and extreme. 'B' also stands for the basic attitudes that the client would hold if they responded healthily to the adversity. These attitudes would be flexible and non-extreme. My practice is to assess both sets of attitudes at the same time. I will explain why later in this principle.
- 'C' = The consequences of holding the basic attitudes at 'B'. There are three sets of consequences that I am interested in: emotional, behavioural and cognitive.

When the client holds a set of rigid and extreme attitudes at 'B' towards the adversity at 'A', then at 'C' their major emotion will be negative and unhealthy, their behaviour will be unconstructive, and their subsequent thinking will tend to be highly distorted and skewed to the negative and ruminative in nature. By contrast, if the client were to hold a set of flexible and non-extreme attitudes towards the same adversity, their major emotion will be negative and healthy. Their behaviour will be constructive, and their subsequent thinking will tend to be realistic, balanced and non-ruminative in nature.

## The 'Situational ABC' Framework in Action

In *Principle 3*, I introduced you to Carl, who sought help for anxiety about speaking in public. I will now show how I helped Carl to assess an example of his nominated problem.

---

[8] When necessary I use the term 'basic attitude' instead of attitude to indicate 'B' in the 'ABC' framework (see Dryden, 2016).

### Selecting a Suitable Example of the Nominated Problem to Assess

Problem assessment is enhanced when the client provides a suitable example of their nominated problem. Such an example should represent the general problem and should be sufficiently memorable for the client to provide useful information. My view is that if my client and I can work with an imminent example of the nominated problem, this will help in two ways. First, the client is preoccupied with the upcoming situation, so is likely to provide the therapist with emotionally-relevant information. Second, it is easier to help the client deal with the imminent situation effectively if this has been the subject of assessment than if a previous example of the problem has been assessed and relevant data carried forward to the upcoming situation.

### Getting a Brief Description of the Relevant 'Situation'

It is useful for the therapist to ask the client to briefly describe the 'situation' in which the problem occurred or is predicted to occur. Carl's selected example was an upcoming 'situation' in which he was going to give a talk at a local school to sixth-form students about a career in accountancy during a careers fair.

### Assessing the Problem-Related 'C'

As mentioned above, 'C' represents the person's responses to the adversity at 'A'. These responses are emotive, behavioural and cognitive[9] in nature. At this point, I will begin with the client's problem-related emotional 'C'. The client may already have told the therapist this when nominating their problem,[10] but it is still important that the therapist identifies the client's emotional 'C' in the selected example.

In my experience, clients present with eight major emotional problems. As I mentioned in *Principle 1*, these problematic emotions are known as unhealthy negative emotions (UNEs). These emotions are anxiety, depression, guilt, shame, hurt and the unhealthy forms of anger, jealousy and envy.

A client may experience more than one UNE in the selected example, and if this is the case, it is important that the client chooses their most problematic emotion. Once they have done that, I help them identify the behaviour and, if relevant, the thinking that accompanies the designated UNE.

In Carl's case, he said that he was anxious about giving a talk to a group of sixth form students about accountancy. His behaviour was to overprepare for his presentation, and his thinking was focused on the students sniggering about his talk after he finished it.

---

[9] Most REB therapists only assess the client's emotions and behaviours. While I do not routinely identify problem-related cognitive 'Cs', I will do so, if it is clear that these are a major feature of the client's problem.

[10] Carl told me that his nominated problem was 'anxiety when speaking in public when attention was on him'.

### Identifying the Adversity at 'A'

Over the years, I have experimented with several ways of helping my client identify the adversity at 'A' in the chosen example of their nominated problem. The most efficient of these methods is what I call 'Windy's Magic Question' (WMQ). The purpose of this method is for the client to be helped or to help themself to identify the adversity or 'A' as quickly as possible (i.e. what the client is most disturbed about) once their unhealthy negative emotion at 'C' has been assessed, and the 'situation' in which 'C' has occurred has been identified and briefly described. Here, I will show how I used this method with Carl.

WINDY'S MAGIC QUESTION

**Step 1**. I asked Carl to focus on his disturbed emotional 'C' (here, 'anxiety').

**Step 2**: I then asked him to focus on the situation in which 'C' occurred (here 'giving a talk on accountancy to a group of sixth-form students at a careers fair').

**Step 3**: Next, I asked Carl: *'Which ingredient could I give you to eliminate or significantly reduce 'C'?'* (here, anxiety). (In this case, Carl said 'my mind not going blank'.) At this point, I took care that Carl did not change the situation (i.e. he did not say something like 'not giving the talk').

**Step 4**: The opposite was probably Carl's adversity or 'A' (which was in Carl's words 'my mind going blank while giving the talk'), but I checked to see if this was the case. I asked: *'So when you think of giving the talk on accountancy to the group of sixth-formers at the careers fair, were you most anxious about your mind going blank?'* Carl said 'yes'. If not, I would use the question again until Carl confirmed what he was most anxious about in the described situation.

## Identifying the Goal-Related at 'C'

At this point, it is a good idea to help the client to set a goal at 'C' concerning the adversity at 'A'. This means helping the client to identify a healthy negative emotion (HNE) alternative to their UNE that features in their unhealthy response to the adversity, a constructive behavioural response and a more balanced, realistic and non-ruminative form of thinking at 'C'. In Carl's case, this appears in Table 4.1.

**Table 4.1** Carl's Problematic Responses and Healthy Goals at 'C'

| 'A' = Mind going blank during presentation | |
|---|---|
| Unhealthy responses at 'C' | Goals (healthy responses at 'C') |
| Emotional 'C' = Anxiety | Emotional goal = Un-anxious concern |
| Behavioural 'C' = Overprepare for the presentation | Behavioural goal = Prepare for the talk without overpreparing it |
| Thinking 'C' = Students sniggering about the talk after I have finished it | Thinking goal = Some students may snigger about the talk after I have finished it, but most probably won't |

### Identifying the Basic Attitudes at 'B'

There are several ways that the REB therapist can help the client identify both the attitudes that underpin their unhealthy responses to the adversity featured in their nominated problem and the attitudes that underpin their potential healthy responses towards the same adversity. I developed a technique called 'Windy's Review Assessment Procedure' (WRAP) which enables the therapist to do this. It also helps the client to see the links between these attitudes and the unhealthy negative emotion (UNE) that features in their disturbed response to the adversity at 'A' (i.e. their problem) and the healthy negative emotion that features in the healthy response to the same adversity (i.e. their goal).

*Windy's Review Assessment Procedure (WRAP):* This technique follows on from Windy's Magic Question (WMQ) method that I illustrated above. Its purpose is as follows. Once the client's adversity at 'A' has been identified (in Carl's case 'going blank during the presentation') and their problem-related and goal-related emotional 'Cs' have been assessed (e.g. 'anxiety' and 'un-anxious concern'), the WRAP helps me identify both the client's rigid attitude and flexible alterative attitude at 'B' and help the client understand the two relevant 'B–C' connections. This technique can also be used with any of the three extreme and non-extreme attitude pairings (i.e. awfulising attitude vs non-awfulising attitude; discomfort intolerance attitude vs discomfort tolerance attitude; devaluation attitude vs unconditional acceptance attitude. I will use the case of Carl to illustrate the use of the WRAP.

**1:**  The therapist informs the client that they are going to review what they know and don't know so far.

> *Windy:*   Let's review what we know and what we don't
>            know so far. OK?
>
> *Carl:*    OK.

**2:**  The therapist tells the client that they both know four things so far. The client's problem-related 'C', their goal-related 'C', the adversity at 'A' and what is important to them which is the part of their attitude that is common to both their rigid attitude and their flexible attitude (see *Principle 1*).

> *Windy:*  We know four things. First, we know that you
>           experience anxiety (problem-related 'C'). Second,
>           we know that you are anxious about your mind
>           going blank during the presentation you are going
>           to give on accountancy to the sixth formers at the
>           careers fair ('A'). Third, we know that your
>           emotional goal is to feel 'un-anxious concern'
>           about the prospect of this happening. Finally, and
>           this is an educated guess on my part, we know that
>           it is important to you that your mind does not go
>           blank during the presentation. Am I correct about
>           these four aspects?
>
> *Carl:*   Quite correct.

[*Note that what I have done here is to identify the part of Carl's attitude (the 'preference component' that is common to both his rigid attitude and his alternative flexible attitude, as we will see.*]

**3:**  Now, tell the client that you are going to try and discover what you don't know, i.e. in this case which attitude underpins his anxiety and non-anxious concern.[11]

> *Windy*:  Now let's review what we don't know. This is where I need your help. We don't know on which of two attitudes your anxiety is based. So, when you are anxious about your mind going when giving a talk to the sixth formers is your anxiety based on Attitude 1: 'It is important to me that my mind doesn't go blank when I am giving the talk and therefore it absolutely must do so' ('Rigid attitude') or Attitude 2: 'It is important to me that my mind doesn't go blank when I am giving the talk boss, but that doesn't mean that it must not do so' ('Flexible attitude')?
>
> *Carl*:  My anxiety is definitely based on Attitude number 1.

**4:**  If necessary, the therapist helps the client that their UNE is based on their rigid attitude if they are unsure.

**5:**  Once the client is clear that their UNE is based on their rigid attitude, the therapist makes and emphasises the rigid attitude-unhealthy 'C' connection.

---

[11] Strictly speaking the REB therapist knows this on theoretical grounds, but the client doesn't.

*Windy:* So, let's see if we can add this point to what we know. Can you see that your anxiety is based on your rigid attitude that it is important to you that your mind doesn't go blank while giving your talk to the sixth formers, and therefore it absolutely must not do so?

*Carl:* Yes, I can see that.

Then the therapist asks the client how they would feel if they really believed their alternative flexible attitude. This is the flexible attitude-healthy 'C' connection.

*Windy:* Now let's suppose instead that you had a firm conviction in Attitude 2, how would you feel about your mind going blank during the talk if you firmly held the attitude that while it was important to you that your mind did not go blank, but that doesn't mean that it must not do so?'

*Carl:* I'd still feel concerned about it,

*Windy:* If you remember this was the goal that we spoke about earlier, isn't it?

*Carl:* That's right.

[*In Carl's case, I had already helped him to see that un-anxious concern was an emotional goal he could aim for about his mind going blank instead of anxiety. This method allows Carl to know that he can achieve his goal by changing his attitude as will be emphasised later.*]

**6:** If necessary, the therapist helps the client to nominate a healthy negative emotion, if not immediately volunteered, and makes and emphasises the flexible attitude-healthy 'C' connection.

7: The therapist helps the client to understand clearly the differences between the two B–C connections.

> *Windy:*  So which attitude underpins which emotion?
> *Carl:*    My anxiety is based on the rigid attitude and the feelings of un-anxious concern is based on the flexible attitude.

8: If the therapist has not already done so, they should now take the opportunity to help the client set the healthy negative emotion as the emotional goal in this situation. If they have already done this, they should remind the client of this fact. In both cases, the therapist encourages the client to see that developing conviction in their flexible attitude is the best way of achieving this goal.

> *Windy:* Do you recall that we already decided that aiming for un-anxious concern was a healthy alternative emotion to anxiety in this case?
> *Carl:*   Yes, I do.
> *Windy:* So, what do you need to do to achieve un-anxious concern?
> *Carl:*   Practise the attitude that while it is important to me that my mind does not go blank during this talk and other talks I may give, it does not mean that this must not happen.

While I have illustrated the WRAP with the client's rigid vs flexible attitude, as I mentioned earlier the therapist can use this technique with any of the extreme vs non-extreme attitude pairings (i.e. awfulising attitude vs non-awfulising attitude; discomfort intolerance attitude vs discomfort tolerance attitude; and devaluation attitude vs unconditional acceptance attitude).

## Reviewing the Work

By this point, the therapist and the client have completed assessing the specific example of the client's nominated problem and the healthy alternative to this problem. This would be a good time for the therapist to encourage the client to stand back and review the work they have done in the assessment of this example. A good way of doing this is for them to consider a visual representation of this work. The therapist may have already done this by using the 'ABC framework' on a whiteboard. If so, all the therapist needs to do is invite the client to consider the whole picture and make any changes before proceeding. If the therapist has not done this, now would be a good time to do so. Table 4.2 presents the 'Situational ABC. Framework' which lists all the factors relevant to the assessment of Carl's problem and his problem-related goal.

**Table 4.2**    Carl's 'Situational ABC' Assessment of a Specific Example of His Nominated Problem and His Problem-Related Goal

| **Situation** = Giving a talk to a group of sixth formers on accountancy at a careers fair | |
|---|---|
| **Adversity ('A')** =My mind will go blank | |
| **Basic attitudes ('B')**<br><br>**(Rigid and extreme)** | **Basic attitudes ('B')**<br><br>**(Flexible and non-extreme)** |
| *Rigid* = I would prefer my mind not to go blank and therefore it must not do so | *Flexible* = I would prefer my mind not to blank, but that does not mean that it must not do so |
| *Extreme (Self-devaluation)* = If my mind goes blank, I would be a fool. | *Non-extreme (unconditional self-acceptance)* = If my mind goes blank, it would not prove that I am a fool. It would prove that I am a fallible human being capable of sensible and foolish things |
| **Consequences ('C')**<br><br>**(Unhealthy and unconstructive)** | **Goals ('G')**<br><br>**(Healthy and constructive)** |
| *Emotional* = Anxiety | *Emotional* = Un-anxious concern |
| *Behavioural* = Overpreparing for the talk | *Behavioural* = Preparing, but not overpreparing for the talk |
| *Thinking* = If my mind goes blank the students will snigger about the talk after I have finished it | *Thinking* = If my mind goes blank, some students may snigger about the talk after I have finished it, but most probably won't |

## From the Specific to the General

After the REB therapist has helped the client to assess a specific example of their nominated problem and helped them to deal with it (see *Principle 5*) they will first encourage the client to assess other examples of the same problem and then examples of other problems that the client wants to deal with in therapy. During the process, both the therapist and client may identify general patterns in the problems and examples that may lead them to conclude that the client has a core rigid/extreme attitude which accounts for the problems. Thus, it turned out that Carl had a core rigid/extreme attitude as follows: 'I don't want to display flaws in public, and therefore I must not do so. If I do, I am defective.' I helped Carl develop the following alternative core flexible/non-extreme attitude, 'I don't want to display flaws in public, but that does not mean that I must not do so. If I do, it will not prove that I am defective. It would prove that I am a fallible, complex human being capable of performing well and poorly in public.'

*

In the next principle, I will discuss how the REB therapist helps the client change specific and core rigid/non-extreme attitudes to their healthy specific and core flexible/non-extreme attitudinal equivalents. I will also discuss other forms of change that the REB therapist promotes when attitude change is not feasible.

## From the Specific to the General.

# Principle 5

# Promoting and Favouring Attitude Change: But Doing So Flexibly

As should be apparent by now, REBT is an *attitude-based approach to therapy*. In Principle 4, I outlined the 'Situational ABC' framework, which clarifies that people are not disturbed by the adversities that face (or think they face); instead, people disturb themselves about these adversities by the rigid and extreme attitudes that they hold towards them. The framework also stresses that if people want to respond healthily to the adversities above, they need to hold flexible and non-extreme attitudes towards them. Thus, from an REBT perspective, the therapist needs to help the client achieve their therapeutic goals by promoting attitude change.

Consequently, in this principle, I will focus on attitude. However, when promoting attitude change in REBT is not possible, the therapist needs to help the client achieve other types of change. I will discuss inferential change, frame change, behavioural change and environmental change.

## Promoting Attitude Change

Ellis (1963) made an important distinction between intellectual insight and emotional insight. He argued that having *intellectual insight* into an idea means that a person understands it, agrees with it but does not fully believe it with the consequence that the new concept has little impact on their feelings and behaviour. By contrast, when the person has emotional insight into an idea the person does fully believe it with the result that it has a significant impact on their feelings and behaviour.

Concerning REBT, this means that initially, the client is likely to have 'intellectual insight' into the idea that holding a flexible/non-extreme in the face of the adversity that is featured in their problem is better for them than holding a rigid/extreme attitude towards the same adversity. However, that is the first phase of attitude change. Intellectual change is vital in REBT, but it is not sufficient to help the client achieve their therapeutic goal, which in this case is responding healthily to adversity. For this to happen, the client will need to engage in several activities designed to promote attitude change and to do so with regularity to enable such change to take place. In what follows, I will first consider how the REB therapist can promote intellectual insight in a client and then consider how emotional insight can be facilitated.

### Promoting Intellectual Insight in REBT

Traditionally, the method that the REB therapist employs to encourage intellectual insight into the reasons why holding rigid/extreme attitudes are problematic for the client why holding flexible/non-extreme attitudes are constructive for them has been called 'disputing'. I do not like the term 'disputing' attitudes because it means to engage the client in an argument with respect to their attitudes and especially to argue irritably. Also, it means to oppose, an idea that does not suggest collaborative working that is important in REBT. Consequently, I prefer the term 'examining' attitudes. This means to inquire closely or to test by questioning to determine knowledge. To preserve the letter 'D' in the extended 'ABCD' framework, I use the term 'dialectical examination' of a client's attitudes. Here 'dialectical' means resolving opposing viewpoints through reasoned arguments, which is a good description of the purpose of examining attitudes in REBT.

However, I drop the term 'dialectical' when I am not referring to this extended framework.

*Dialectical Examination of Attitudes:* While there are different ways in which an REB therapist can engage their client in the attitude examination process, I favour one where the therapist presents both attitudes (i.e. rigid vs flexible or extreme vs non-extreme) to the client who is asked to examine them both at the same time and asked to choose (1) which is true and which is false, (2) which is logical and which is illogical, and (3) which is helpful and which is unhelpful. After providing each answer, the client is invited to give reasons for their choice. This explains why I call this my 'choice-based' method of examining attitudes because a rigid or extreme attitude is diametrically opposed[12] to their flexible or non-extreme alternative. Table 5.1

---

[12] It is important to note that, for example, a rigid attitude and its flexible alternative, do not exist on a continuum but are diametrically opposite. Although both are based on a preference (e.g. 'I want you to like me....) when the person makes this rigid they assert a demand (e.g. '.... and therefore you have to do so'), but when they keep this preference flexible they negate the demand (e.g. '....but you don't have to like me'). Asserting and negating a demand are opposite processes. This same analysis can also be applied to all three of the extreme attitudes and their non-extreme alternatives.

presents my method of doing this, which I call 'Windy's Choice-Based Method of Examining Attitudes' and Table 5.2 presents how I applied this with Carl.

**Table 5.1**    'Windy's Choice-Based Method of Examining Attitudes': Instructions for Use

1.  The therapist has the client focus on their rigid attitude and their flexible attitude[13]

2.  The therapist asks the client which attitude is true and which is false and to give reasons for their choice

3.  The therapist asks the client which attitude is logical and which illogical false and to give reasons for their choice

4.  The therapist asks the client which attitude is helpful and which unhelpful and to give reasons for their choice

5.  The therapist asks the client which attitude they would teach their children and to give reasons for their choice

6.  The therapist asks the client to which attitude they wish to commit themself going forward and to give reasons for their choice

7.  The therapist asks the client to voice any doubts, reservations they have about their decision and deals with their responses

Before using this method or any other way of helping a client examine their attitudes, the REB therapist needs to explain what they are about to do and see if the client has any

[13] These steps also apply to the examination of any of the extreme and non-extreme attitudes

questions before proceeding. Please note before looking at Table 5.2 that I did this with Carl.

**Table 5.2**    Using 'Windy's Choice-Based Method of Examining Attitudes' with Carl

1.    I focused Carl his rigid attitude and their flexible attitude.

*Windy:*    OK let's focus on your two attitudes, Attitude A: 'I would prefer my mind not to go blank and therefore it must not do so' and Attitude B: 'I would prefer my mind not to blank, but that does not mean that it must not do so.'[14] I am going to ask you a number of questions designed to help you to examine these attitudes and help you to decide which attitude you want to cast aside and which you want to forward with. OK?
*Carl:*    OK.

2.    I asked Carl which attitude is true and which is false and to give reasons for his choice

*Windy*:    Which of these two attitudes is true and which one is false?
*Carl*:    Attitude A is false and Attitude B is false.
*Windy*:    What are your reasons?
*Carl*:    Well, Attitude A is false because, I don't have to get my desires met. Just because I don't want my mind to go blank doesn't mean that it must not do so. Attitude B is true because it recognises this fact.

3.    I asked Carl which attitude is logical and which illogical false and to give reasons for his choice.

*Windy*:    Which of these two attitudes is logical and which one is illogical?
*Carl*:    Attitude A is illogical and Attitude B is logical.
*Windy*:    What are your reasons?
*Carl*:    Well, it makes no logical sense for me to conclude that just because I don't want my mind not to go blank therefore it must not. My desire is not rigid but my demand is rigid and you can't logically derive

*Table 5.2 continued*

---

[14] I suggest that the therapist write these attitudes down on separate pieces of paper so that the client can read them during the method.

something rigid from something that is not rigid. On the other hand Attitude B is logical because its two components are not rigid and can be logically connected.

4.    I asked Carl which attitude is helpful and which unhelpful and to give reasons for his choice.

*Windy*:    Which of these two attitudes is helpful and which one is unhelpful?
*Carl*:    Attitude A is unhelpful and Attitude B is helpful.
*Windy*:    What are your reasons?
*Carl:*    Attitude A is unhelpful because it leads to anxiety and increases the chances that my mind will go blank. Attitude B is helpful because it it does not try to exclude the possibility that my mind will go blank and calms me down as a result.

5.    I asked Carl which attitude he would teach his children and to give reasons for their choice.

*Windy*:    Which attitude would you teach your children?
*Carl*:    Attitude B.
*Windy*:    Why?
*Carl*:    Because I would not want them to suffer as I have and Attitude B would not lead to suffering. It would lead to concern and that is much healthier. Also, Attitude reflects reality and I would want my kids to adopt a realistic outlook.

6.    I asked Carl to which attitude he wished to commit himself going forward and to give reasons for his choice.

*Windy*:    So, which of these two attitudes do you want to commit to going forward?
*Carl*:    Attitude B.
*Windy*:    Why?
*Carl*:    It's a no brainer. It's helpful, true and makes sense while Attitude B is the opposite.

7.    I asked Carl to voice any doubts, reservations or objections he had about his responses and I dealt with his responses

*Windy*:    Do you have any doubts, reservations about going forward with Attitude B?
*Carl*:    Only what that would involve.
*Windy*:    I'll explain that soon.

## Promoting Emotional Insight in REBT

As I said earlier, emotional insight in REBT occurs when the client has a deep conviction in flexible and non-extreme attitudes to the extent that it has a significant constructive impact on their emotions, behaviour and subsequent thinking.

*Acting in Ways that Are Consistent with Developing Flexible/Non-Extreme Attitudes:* In my view, the best way that the client can achieve emotional insight is to act regularly in ways that are consistent with their flexible and non-extreme attitudes and inconsistent with their rigid and extreme attitudes. It is important that the client does this while facing the adversities that feature in their problems. The best way the client can do this is to use the principle of 'challenging, but not overwhelming' (Dryden, 1985). This means that the client chooses to face a particular adversity that is challenging for them to face at the time, but not overwhelming. In following this principle, what the client finds initially 'overwhelming', they will later find challenging and thus be able to do. The therapist here also needs to encourage the client to face such adversities even though they may be uncomfortable or unconfident in doing so. When clients believe that they must have the presence of such internal states as comfort or confidence before they face relevant adversities, then they will not face them and will therefore not experience appropriate change. Consequently, the therapist needs to help the client identify and deal with such obstacles to attitude change.

In REBT, the therapist generally begins by helping the client to change their specific rigid/extreme attitudes related to the example of their nominated problem first selected. Thus, I encouraged Carl to give talks whenever he thought that his mind might go blank. If relevant, the therapist encourages the client to face other situations that might approximate the same adversity. In particular, the therapist and client look for themes that represent the adversities first discussed by the client. Then the therapist encourages the client to face other examples of the theme while rehearsing relevant flexible/non-extreme attitudes. Here, I helped Carl identify the theme of public displays of behaviour that fell short of this ideal. Besides being anxious about his mind going blank, Carl was anxious about not answering questions when called upon to do so in work meetings and saying the wrong things at parties. I first encouraged Carl to complete my Dryden REBT Form (DRF)[15] on each of these problems (see Table 5.3) before encouraging him to seek out situations where the adversities may occur while holding in mind the flexible/non-extreme attitudes that he was endeavouring to develop.

In the previous principle, I discussed how the REB therapist could help the client identify any relevant core rigid/extreme attitudes. These are attitudes that they hold in a variety of 'adversity-similar' situations. I mentioned that Carl had a core rigid/extreme attitude as follows: 'I don't want to display flaws in public, and therefore I must not do so. If I do, I am defective.' I helped Carl develop the following alternative core flexible/non-extreme attitude, 'I don't want to display flaws in public, but that does not mean that I must not do so. If I do, it

---

[15] The DRF is my own example of the ABC-based self-help form that REB therapists use in REBT.

will not prove that I am defective. It would prove that I am a fallible, complex human being capable of performing well and poorly in public.'

**Table 5.3**    The Dryden REBT Form (DRF)

| **Situation =** | |
| --- | --- |
| **Adversity ('A') =** | |
| Basic attitudes ('B')<br>(rigid and extreme)<br><br>*Rigid =*<br><br>*Extreme =* | Basic attitudes ('B')<br>(flexible and non-extreme)<br><br>*Flexible =*<br><br>*Non-Extreme =* |
| Consequences ('C')<br>(Unhealthy and unconstructive)<br><br>*Emotional =*<br><br>*Behavioural =*<br><br>*Thinking =* | Goals ('G')<br>(Healthy and constructive)<br><br>*Emotional =*<br><br>*Behavioural =*<br><br><br>*Thinking =* |

1.  Write down a brief, objective description of the *situation* you were in.

2.  Identify your '*C*' – your major disturbed emotion, your unconstructive behaviour and, if relevant, your distorted and/or ruminative subsequent thinking.

3.  Identify your '*A*' – this is what you were most disturbed about in the situation.

    (Steps 2 and 3 are interchangeable.)

4.  Set emotional, behavioural and thinking goals at '*G*'.

5.  Identify your rigid/extreme basic attitude i.e. rigid attitude + awfulising attitude, discomfort intolerance attitude or devaluation attitude.

6.  Identify the alternative flexible/non-extreme basic attitudes that will enable you to achieve your goals, i.e. flexible attitude + non-awfulising attitude, discomfort tolerance attitude or unconditional acceptance. attitude

OVERLEAF

7.  Examine (at '*D*') both your rigid/extreme attitudes and flexible/non-extreme attitudes and choose one set to operate on. Give reasons for your choice. Which set would you teach a group of children, for example and why? Remember that you are choosing attitudes that will help you to achieve your emotional, behavioural and thinking goals. The effects of dialectical examination (or '*E*')should also be your goals at *G*.

8.  List the actions you are going to take to achieve your goals.

9.  Examine '*A*' and consider how realistic it was. Given all the facts, would there have been a more realistic way of looking at '*A*'? - if so, write it down.

'D' (Dialectical examination) =

Taking action =

Examine 'A' =

While using the theme-based approach to promoting the attitude discussed above, the therapist urges the client to take the adversities that feature in their problem and seek out these adversities while using relevant specific examples of their developing flexible/non-extreme attitude. While using the core attitude-based approach to promoting such change, the therapist encourages the client to rehearse their core flexible/non-extreme attitudes while facing the same adversities. My view is that when used together, the theme-based and core attitude-based approaches are compelling. For example, whenever Carl went to a party, he reminded himself that if he said the wrong, he could accept himself both for saying the wrong thing at the party (theme-based approach) and for revealing a flaw in public (core attitude-based approach).

*Imagery Rehearsal:* When encouraging the client to use their imagery modality to promote attitude change, the REB therapist suggests that the client imagine that their adversity has occurred and asks the client to rehearse their flexible/non-extreme attitude while facing the adversity in their mind's eye. The client can do this before facing the situation in which the adversity may occur or when not facing the situation. As an example of the former, before giving his talk to the group of sixth formers, Carl closed his eyes and pictured his mind going blank and saw himself dealing with this while holding his flexible and non-extreme attitude. As an example of the latter, the client can use a technique known as 'rational-emotive imagery' (see Table 5.4). In this method, the client practises changing their unhealthy negative emotion to its healthy negative emotional equivalent in a specific imagined episode of their problem. As described in Table 5.4, the therapist encourages the client to make this shift by changing their specific rigid/extreme attitude to the alternative specific flexible/non-extreme attitude. They can be asked to do this several times a day as it does not involve imagery rehearsal before facing, in reality, the situation in which the adversity may occur.

Some clients argue that if they imagine that the adversity will occur and practice dealing with it while holding their flexible/non-extreme attitude in their mind's eye, it makes it more likely that the adversity will happen. By contrast, they hold that if they think that the adversity won't happen, it won't happen. If a client says this, I suggest that the REB therapist responds in two ways. First, the therapist can ask the client how this works. If Carl assumes that his mind won't go blank while giving his talk to a group of sixth formers, does this mean that his mind will not go blank? In which case, does this mean that all he has to do is make that assumption to solve his problem? Second, the therapist can ask the client how assuming that the adversity will not occur helps the person deal effectively with the adversity should it happen. Carl recognised that this wouldn't help him. Furthermore, he also realised that even if using imagery rehearsal did increase the chances of his mind going blank in the situation when he gave his talk to the group of sixth formers, he would be prepared for this eventuality.

**Table 5.4**    Helping the Client to Use Rational-Emotive Imagery

1.  The therapist asks the client to take a situation in which they disturbed themself and has them focus on the aspect of the situation they were most disturbed about (i.e. the adversity).

2.  The therapist asks the client to close their eyes and imagine the situation as vividly as possible and focus on the adversity.

3.  The therapist suggests that the client allows themself to really experience the unhealthy negative emotion that they felt at the time while still focusing intently on the adversity. The therapist ensures that their unhealthy negative emotion is <u>one</u> of the following: anxiety, depression, shame, guilt, hurt, unhealthy anger, unhealthy jealousy, unhealthy envy.

4.  The therapist encourages the client to really experience this disturbed emotion for a moment or two and then change their emotional response to a healthy negative emotion while all the time focusing intently on the adversity within the chosen situation. The therapist urges the client not to change the intensity of the emotion, just the emotion. Thus, if their original unhealthy negative emotion was anxiety, the therapist asks them to change this to concern; if it was depression, change it to sadness. The therapist suggests that they change shame to disappointment, guilt to remorse, hurt to sorrow, unhealthy anger to healthy anger, unhealthy jealousy to healthy jealousy and unhealthy envy to healthy envy. Again, the therapist urges them to change the unhealthy negative emotion to its healthy equivalent, but to keep the level of intensity of the new emotion as strong as the old emotion. The therapist asks them to keep experiencing this new emotion for about five minutes, all the time focusing on the adversity. If they go back to the old, unhealthy negative emotion, the therapist asks them to bring the new healthy negative emotion back.

5.  At the end of five minutes, the therapist asks the client how they changed their emotion.

6.  The therapist makes sure that the client changed their emotional response by changing their specific rigid/non-extreme attitude to its healthy flexible/non-extreme alternative. If they did not do so (if, for example, they changed their emotion by changing the adversity to make it less negative or neutral or by holding an indifference attitude towards the adversity), the therapist asks them to do the exercise again and to keep doing this until they have changed their emotion only by changing their specific rigid/non-extreme attitude to its healthy flexible/non-extreme attitudinal alternative.

*Emotively-based Cognitive Techniques:* The purpose of emotionally-based cognitive methods is to allow the client to invest emotionally in the flexible/non-extreme attitudes they wish to develop. I will discuss two of these techniques: (1) the zig-zag technique and (2) forceful flexible/non-extreme attitudinal self-statements.

**1. The zig-zag technique.** The purpose of the zig-zag technique is to allow the client to respond to their own attacks on their developing flexible/non-extreme attitude and to do so with emotional engagement. I will first describe how the REB therapist can encourage the client to complete a 'written zig-zag form' (see Figure 5.1).

- The therapist asks the client to write down their core or specific flexible/non-extreme attitude in the top left-hand box.

- Then, the therapist asks them to rate their present level of conviction in this attitude on a 100% point scale with 0% = no conviction and 100% = total conviction (i.e. they believe it in their heart, and it would markedly influence their feelings and behaviour). The therapist asks the client to write down this rating in the space provided on the form.

- The therapist suggests that the client attack this flexible/non-extreme attitude. They are told to put their attack in the form of a doubt, reservation or objection to this flexible/non-extreme attitude. It should also contain an explicit rigid/extreme attitude. The therapist asks the client to make this attack as genuine as possible and write it down in the first box on the right.

Flexible / non-extreme attitude

Rating of conviction =     %

Response

Response

Response

Attack

Attack

Attack

Rating of conviction of original
flexible / non-extreme attitude =     %

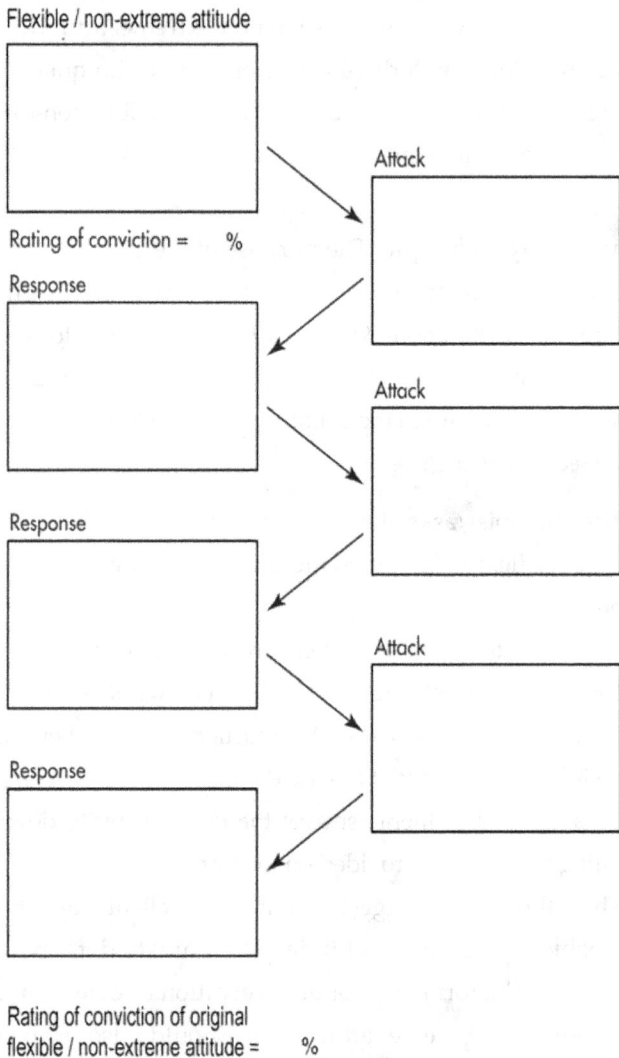

**Figure 5.1**   Written Zig-Zag Form

- Then, the therapist asks the client to respond to this attack as fully, persuasively and emotionally as they can. The therapist tells them that it is vital that they respond to each element of the attack. In particular, the client is asked to ensure that they respond to rigid/extreme attitude statements and also to distorted or unrealistic inferences framed in the form of a doubt, reservation or objection to the flexible/non-extreme attitude. The client is asked to write down their response in the second box on the right.

- The therapist suggests that the client continues in this vein until they have answered all their attacks and cannot think of any more. The therapist asks the client to focus on the flexible/non-extreme attitude they are trying to strengthen throughout this process.

- When the client has answered all of their attacks, the therapist asks them to re-rate their conviction level in the flexible/non-extreme attitude using the 0–100% scale as before. If they have followed the instructions above, then their rating will have gone up appreciably.

Once the client has become proficient at using the written zig-zag form, the therapist can suggest that they use the 'recorded zig-zag method'. The purpose of this variation is the same as in the written zig-zag: for the client to strengthen their conviction in their developing core and/or specific flexible/non-extreme attitudes by responding persuasively and emotionally to attacks on them. However, rather than writing down the dialogue, the client speaks them onto a digital voice recorder or a voice recording 'app' on their smartphone. As the client uses spoken language in this variation, the therapist can suggest that they vary their voice tone and the forcefulness of their spoken words to aid them in this process. The therapist should remind the client that they need to be as emotionally engaged as they can be in this technique, the purpose of which is to increase their level of conviction in the developing core or specific flexible/non-extreme attitude.

**2. Forceful flexible/non-extreme attitudinal self-statements.** Once a client has developed a flexible/non-extreme attitude, the REB therapist can encourage them to come up with a shortened version of this attitude to repeat to themself in a forceful way that fully engages their emotions. They can rehearse this 'self-statement' at any time, but especially before, during and after facing a situation in which their adversity may occur. The self-statement may reflect a specific flexible/non-extreme attitude (e.g. 'I am fallible if my mind goes blank') or a core flexible/non-extreme attitude (e.g. 'I'm not immune from revealing flaws. Nobody is!'). The point is that the client needs to be encouraged to invest their emotions while repeating it to themself.

## Promoting Other Forms of Change

Suppose the client is unable or unwilling to change their rigid/extreme attitude to their alternative flexible/non-extreme attitude. In that case, the REB therapist is flexible enough to suggest other forms of change to the client.

### Promoting Inferential Change

Promoting inferential change involves the therapist helping the client change the inference that they have made at 'A' rather than the basic attitudes they hold towards this adversity. Let me present an example. Many years ago, Richard Wessler, who used to be Director of Training at the Albert Ellis Institute, told me of a woman who consulted him because she felt unhealthily angry at her father, who she said was overly intrusive into her life. Wessler began by helping the woman understand that she held a set of rigid/extreme attitudes towards her father's intrusiveness. If she were to examine and change it to an alternative set of flexible/non-extreme attitudes, she would experience healthy anger towards this adversity. However, the woman was not interested in Wessler's strategy but still wanted to deal with her anger.

Thinking on his feet, Wessler asked his client what her father did that she found so intrusive. She replied, 'He asks me, "Noo what's doing?" It makes me so mad!' Wessler then asked his client, how often she has heard her father ask people, 'Noo, what's doing?' The client replied that her father had used that phrase every time he begins a conversation with someone. Wessler then inquired of the client if it were possible that when her father asked her 'Noo, what's doing?' that he was just opening a conversation with her rather than being overly intrusive into her life. The woman then realised that her inference was mistaken and that her father was not excessively intrusive into her life, and consequently, she lost her anger.

Wessler was aware that if the client later had evidence that her father was overly intrusive into her life that she would once again experience unhealthy anger due to her rigid/extreme attitudes, but she was happy with his intervention. From her perspective, her problem was solved.

In this example, the frame had not changed. The woman's father asked her, 'Noo, what's doing?' However, she changed her inference about this from, 'my father is intruding into my life', which was a negative inference to 'this is how he starts conversations' which was a neutral inference.

### Promoting Frame Change

When a therapist encourages the client to make a frame change, they help the client place adversity into a completely different frame. An excellent example of this comes from a story I once read in *Reader's Digest* that I use as a teaching tool in my REBT training workshops.

A wealthy older woman would periodically book into a penthouse suite in a high-class hotel for a few days' rest and recuperation. When she did so, she insisted on complete quiet with no disruptions of any kind during her visits. On one occasion, she went to her usual suite, changed her clothing and closed her eyes to relax. At that moment, from the adjoining suite, someone began to play the piano. The woman was furious. She had requested complete quiet, and this was being disturbed by the piano playing from the adjoining suite. Immediately, she went down to see the hotel manager and ranted at him for five minutes concerning how her expressed instructions were ignored. After she had finished, she asked the manager what he had to say for himself. Here is how the ensuing conversation went:

| | |
|---|---|
| *Hotel Manager:* | Madam, I appreciate your concerns, but may I ask you a question? |
| *Woman:* | If you must. |
| *Hotel Manager:* | Madam have you heard of ... [and the manager mentioned one of the world's leading pianists]? |
| *Woman:* | Yes, I have. Why? |
| *Hotel Manager:* | Well, madam, he is in town this evening for a one night only concert which has been fully booked for months. |
| *Woman:* | What has that got to do with anything? |
| *Hotel Manager:* | Madam, that man is playing the piano in the next suite to you. Madam, you are getting the rare privilege of a private concert. Madam, quick, back to your room before you miss it. |

At that, the woman went back to her room as quickly as she could, eager to attend her 'private concert'.

What the hotel manager did was put what the woman regarded as an adversity (a disruption to her longed-for peace and quiet) into a different frame (the privilege of a private concert given by a world-renowned pianist). He knew instinctively that the woman would be flattered by the idea of having a private concert given by the pianist and thus he put the adversity into that frame.

As you can see, frame change (as demonstrated above) changes an adversity into something very positive. In contrast, as discussed in the previous example, inference change transforms an adversity into a neutral event.

### Promoting Behavioural Change

When the REB therapist helps the client change their behaviour without changing their attitude, they do so mainly because the client is not interested in or unable to make an attitude change. Such behavioural change has several beneficial results.

*Behavioural change helps the client to deal effectively with an adversity.* An example of this occurs when the therapist helps the client develop a new behavioural skill such as assertiveness. When the client changes their behaviour from non-assertive to assertive in standing up to bullying, for example, they learn to deal effectively with such an adversity by a change in behaviour.

*Behavioural change helps the client to change an inference.* An example of this occurs when the client infers that people will find their conversation boring in social situations. To help with this, the therapist teaches the client conversational skills. When the client has improved their conversational behaviour and uses it in social situations, they discover that others are interested in what they have to say. In doing so, they change their inference that others will find their conversation boring.

*Behavioural change helps the client change their attitude.* An example of this occurs when the client changes their behaviour in the face of an adversity and in doing so, changes their attitude towards the adversity. For example, a client may have avoided socialising with members of the opposite sex because they hold an awfulising attitude towards being rejected by them. If the client changes their behaviour and approaches members of the opposite sex and gets rejected by someone, then they may learn they while being rejected is bad, it is not awful.

## Promoting Environmental Change

While the REB therapist does not generally encourage clients to change their environment in which the adversity is present until they have made an attitude change towards that adversity, there are important exceptions to this principle. For example, suppose a client is at risk because of the environment in which they live (e.g. a domestic abuse situation). In that case, the therapist will encourage the client to leave the situation rather than stay in it and change their attitude before deciding what to do.

*

In this principle, I have argued that the REB therapist favours and promotes attitude change in a client whenever possible, but that REBT is sufficiently flexible to enable the therapist to facilitate other forms of change when indicated. In the following principle, I will discuss the importance of the REB therapist helping the client to identify and articulate their doubts, reservations and objections to any aspect of the REB therapeutic process.

# PRINCIPLE 6

# Dealing with Doubts, Reservations and Objections

As I have outlined so far in this book, REBT has a clear position concerning the factors that account for a client's problems, how they may unwittingly maintain their problems and what they need to do to address them effectively to effect change. Also, the REB therapist is encouraged to make this position explicit at the outset so that the client can determine whether REBT makes sense to them and can potentially benefit them. Once the client has given their informed consent to proceed, this does not mean that the client understands and agrees with all the REBT concepts to which they are likely to be introduced. On the contrary, the client may have some doubts, reservations and objections (DROs) to these concepts going forward. Given this, the REB therapist has a significant set of tasks concerning a client's DROs as detailed below. However, before I discuss these tasks, let me discuss common client doubts, reservations and objections.

## Common Client Doubts, Reservations and Objections (DROs)

As noted above, a client can have a DRO concerning any REBT concept or any aspect of the REB therapeutic process. Here is a partial list of some of the most common DROs that REB therapists encounter in their work.[16]

### DROs about the REBT Concept of Emotional Responsibility

As I discussed in *Principle 1*, REBT is based on the principle of emotional responsibility that states that the client is largely responsible for the emotions they experience towards adversities because of their attitudes towards these adversities. For some clients, this is a liberating idea while for others, it is a threatening one. Thus, some clients think that they are to be blamed for how they feel if they take such responsibility. Others believe that the therapist is blaming them for creating their own disturbed feelings. Given these DROs, the therapist needs to clarify that adversities contribute to but do not create a client's feelings. If the client takes responsibility for their feelings, the therapist does not blame them for doing so, nor should they blame themself.

---

[16] For a fuller discussion of dealing with clients' DROs in REBT see Dryden (2021b).

### DROs about Giving Up Rigid/Extreme Attitudes in Favour of Flexible/Non-Extreme Attitudes

Clients tend to have several DROs about giving up each of the attitudes that underpin their problems and about developing their healthy attitudinal alternatives.

*DROs about Giving Up Rigid Attitudes in Favour of Flexible Attitudes:* A client may be reluctant to let go of their rigid attitude in favour of their flexible attitude because they think that their rigid attitude motivates them and that their flexible attitude alternative doesn't. In response, the therapist needs to help the client see that both attitudes' preference component motivates them. In contrast, the asserted demand component of the rigid attitude interferes with their motivation. The client also needs to see that the negated demand component of their flexible attitude also does not interfere with their motivation (see *Principle 1*, Figure 1.1).

*DROs about Giving Up Awfulising Attitudes in Favour of Non-Awfulising Attitudes:* A client maybe reluctant to let go of their awfulising attitude because they think that what happened to them was 'awful'. Furthermore, they believe that a non-awfulising attitude makes light of what transpired. In response, the therapist needs to help the client to see that 'awful' means that you can never get over this experience. Also, a non-awfulising attitude does not make light of the experience but gives them hope that they can transcend the experience. As I have shown elsewhere, the REB therapist needs to be sensitive when discussing the differences between a non-awfulising attitude and an awfulising attitude, especially in the face of a significant adversity (Dryden, 2020).

*DROs about Giving Up Discomfort Intolerance Attitudes in Favour of Discomfort Tolerance Attitudes:* A common DRO expressed by clients about giving up a discomfort intolerance attitude in favour of a discomfort tolerance attitude is that the latter means passively putting up with an adversity. The REB therapist needs to show the client who holds this DRO that tolerating an adversity helps the person take effective action towards changing the adversity and is the opposite of passively putting up with the situation without attempting to change it.

*DROs about Giving Up Devaluation Attitudes in Favour of Unconditional Acceptance Attitudes:* A common DRO expressed by some clients about giving up a self-devaluation attitude in favour of an unconditional self-acceptance (USA) attitude is that the latter means that the person is complacent and would not seek to change aspects of themselves that they do not like. In contrast, the self-devaluation (SD) attitude promotes such change. The REB therapist should show the client who holds this DRO that the reality is the opposite. In holding a USA attitude, the client acknowledges that they are a complex, unrateable, fallible human being and that acceptance of self does not preclude the person from changing what they don't like about themselves. In fact, this attitude encourages such change, free from the disturbed feelings that stem from an SD attitude which will interfere with the person changing a disliked aspect of themselves.

### DROs about Giving Up UNEs in Favour of HNEs

As I discussed in *Principle 2*, REBT distinguishes between two different emotional responses to adversities: unhealthy negative emotions (UNEs) based on rigid/extreme attitudes and healthy negative emotions (HNEs) based on flexible/non-extreme attitudes. Even when the REB therapist carefully distinguishes between these different emotions, the client may still have DROs about giving up a particular UNE in favour of its HNE alternative. Here are a few examples of such DROs and how the REB therapist needs to respond to them.[17]

***DROs about Giving Up Anxiety in Favour of Concern:*** A client may think that they need their anxiety to motivate them. This is particularly the case with a client who struggles with procrastination. In response, the REB therapist shows the client that the constructive motivational properties of both anxiety and concern come from the preference component common to the rigid and flexible attitudes that underpin these emotions respectively and from the negated demand component of the flexible attitude underpinning concern. By contrast, while the asserted demand component of the rigid attitude may motivate the client, its motivational properties tend to be unconstructive. A headless chicken is motivated to find its head but can't see where it is, given its anxiety.

---

[17] See Dryden (2021b) for a fuller discussion of these DROs as they pertain to all eight UNEs and their HNE alternatives.

***DROs about Giving Up Guilt in Favour of Remorse:*** A client may think that guilt is a healthy response to a violation of their moral code and are thus reluctant to work towards remorse. Here, the REB therapist needs to stress that the self-devaluation attitude in guilt is not healthy and may even lead the person to do more bad things. Thus, when a person regards themself as a bad person, this self-identity leads them to act in ways consistent with 'who they are'. This self-fulfilling feature is not present in remorse since an unconditional self-acceptance attitude underpins it. Here the person acknowledges that they can act, badly and neutrally, whereas the 'I'm bad' attitude in guilt biases the person towards behaving badly.

***DROs about Giving Up Unhealthy Anger in Favour of Healthy Anger:*** When a client's unhealthy anger is righteous ('I am right and good, You are wrong and bad'), the person may be reluctant to give up their unhealthy anger in favour of its healthy alternative because they think that doing so means admitting they are wrong. This is not the case. A person can still believe that they are right, and the other person is wrong without devaluing the other and without aggrandising one's self. Healthy anger enables the client to hold this position and reassures them that in doing so, it does not mean admitting that they are wrong.

### DROs about the REBT Concept of Therapeutic Responsibility

I discussed REBT's emotional responsibility concept ('I am largely responsible for my emotions because of the attitudes that I hold for which I am responsible') in *Principle 1*. REBT's concept of therapeutic responsibility follows on for this ('Since I am largely responsible for my emotions and for the attitudes that underpin them, I am largely responsible for changing my emotions by changing my attitudes').

Sometimes, when a client has been mistreated by another person and has disturbed themself about this, they may be reluctant to assume their therapeutic responsibility. Thus, they may say something like 'I should not be the one to change because I am the blameless victim here. The other person should change.' In response, the REB therapist would point out that the client has a choice to change their emotions or not to do so. If they choose not to do so, the consequence is that they are stuck with their disturbed feelings. If they want to change these feelings, then the only way to do this is to assume therapeutic responsibility and change the attitudes that underpin their disturbed feelings. It is also unlikely that the other person will change since they probably don't feel the need to do so. Here, the REB therapist helps the client see what their options are and the consequences of each option. Then, the therapist invites the client to decide to assume their therapeutic responsibility or not. When the REB therapist takes this tack, the client almost always assumes their therapeutic responsibility and works towards changing their feelings by changing their attitudes. Sometimes the client does this reluctantly to which the therapist should respond with empathic understanding.

## The Therapist's Tasks Concerning the Client's Doubt, Reservation or Objection (DRO)

The REB therapist has several to perform concerning a client's doubts, reservations and objections. These are: (a) explaining what doubts, reservations and objections are and why it is important for a client to disclose them; (b) sensing that the client may be harbouring a DRO; (c) checking this out with them; (d) helping them to formulate their DRO; and (e) responding effectively to the client's DRO until it has been effectively addressed.

### Explaining about DROs

Towards the beginning of therapy when the REB therapist is discussing the nature of REBT with the client and what tasks both have in the process, it is useful for the therapist to alert the client to the possibility that they may have some doubts, reservations or objections to one or more REBT concepts or some aspect of the therapeutic process. If so, the therapist encourages the client to voice these DROs and asks the client for permission to check with them concerning the possible existence of a DRO if they don't mention it.

### Sensing that a Client Holds a DRO

During therapy, the therapist may sense that the client is harbouring a DRO but has not mentioned it yet. In these circumstances, the therapist discerns this from the client's non-verbal or paraverbal behaviour.

### Checking the Existence of a DRO with the Client

If the therapist has identified a possible DRO, then it is important that they address this possibility. For example, the therapist can ask the client directly if they have such a DRO or point to the client behaviour that led the therapist to infer the possible existence of a DRO. Thus, the therapist may say something like, 'I noticed that you pulled a bit of a face when I was talking about the concept unconditional self-acceptance, were you reacting negatively to what I was saying?'

### Helping a Client to Formulate a DRO

Once the client has indicated that they do have a DRO about something the therapist has said, for example, then the therapist needs to help the client to formulate this DRO. In doing this, the therapist should adopt a non-defensive, understanding stance to facilitate this formulation.

### Responding Effectively to a DRO

Once the therapist has helped the client formulate their DRO, they should help them examine it through a mixture of Socratic and didactic interventions until the person's DRO has been assuaged.[18]

*

In the final principle, I will discuss how the REB therapist works with a client's emotional problems, dissatisfaction issues, and wishes to develop themself. I will particularly discuss what to do if a client wishes to discuss all three topics during therapy.

---

[18] See Dryden (2021b, chapter 8) for some examples of how an REB therapist does this with a client.

# PRINCIPLE 7

# Encouraging Movement from Disturbance to Dissatisfaction and Thence to Development, if Necessary: From Therapy to Coaching

A client may seek help from an REB therapist for a variety of reasons. Thus, they may have one or more emotional problems, or they may have one or more practical issues with which they are dissatisfied (but not disturbed) or feel that they can get more out of themself in one or more areas of their life. A client may want help predominantly with a dissatisfaction problem but may also be disturbed about the reason for their dissatisfaction. Or they may seek coaching to develop themself they may also be emotionally disturbed about their failure to fulfil their potential as a person. To complicate matters even more, a client may have all three such issues.

As I have pointed out elsewhere (Dryden, 2021c), a distinctive feature of REBT is that it suggests a particular order in which such problems and issues can be tackled. Thus, the therapist, all things being equal, should invite the client to tackle their emotional problems before their dissatisfaction-based practical problems and after these have been dealt with issues of personal development should be considered. I say here, 'all things being equal' because the client may have a

101

different idea concerning the order in which they would like to deal with their issues, and it may differ from the REBT-suggested order. In such cases, the REB therapist should explain their rationale for the REBT-suggested order, but go with the client if the latter disagree in order to preserve the working alliance between them.

## Disturbance before Dissatisfaction

REBT argues that unless there are good reasons to the contrary, it is best for the therapist to help the client address their emotional problems before their dissatisfaction problems. The reason for this is as follows. Suppose a client addresses a dissatisfaction issue before they deal with their emotional disturbance. In that case, their disturbed feelings will get in the way of their efforts to change directly the adversity about which they are dissatisfied.

Let me provide an example. Harriet is dissatisfied with her sister's choice of friends. However, she is also unhealthily angry about this. Every time she tries to discuss the issue with her sister, she makes herself unhealthily angry about it, shouts at her sister and makes pejorative remarks about her and her friends. Harriet's anger leads to her sister, making herself angry as well, and they get nowhere. Certainly, Harriet's unhealthy anger does not encourage her sister to stand back and look objectively at her friends or to listen to Harriet's genuine concern about the company she is keeping. Harriet's angry behaviour is more likely to lead her sister to become defensive.

In therapy, Harriet's REB therapist encouraged her to deal with her unhealthy anger before her dissatisfaction issue. Her therapist helped Harriet identify, examine and change her rigid demand that her sister must listen to her to a flexible attitude that while it was preferable for her sister to listen to Harriet, she did not have to do so. Because she was displeased, but not unhealthily angry, Harriet was able to express her concern to her sister who listened more openly but still decided to remain friends with the people to whom Harriet objected. Harriet comforted herself that while her sister chose to keep these friends, she, Harriet had fulfilled her sisterly duty and allowed her sister to accept the consequences of her own choices.

## Disturbance before Development

When I was initially trained as a counsellor in the 1970s, the line between counselling and psychotherapy was clearly drawn. Psychotherapy was for people with emotional disturbance and counselling was for people who wanted to develop themselves. Since then, the line between counselling and psychotherapy has become blurred, and for some, the two are indistinguishable. These days, coaching occupies the space previously occupied by counselling and is seen by many as an acceptable way of seeking help. This has meant that people who have emotional problems seek help from coaches who are generally not trained to deal with such issues. However, REB coaches *are* trained to deal with both issues of development and disturbance.

In general, it is challenging for a client to develop themself when they are emotionally disturbed. Focusing on development areas when someone is emotionally disturbed is akin to encouraging that person to climb a very steep hill with hefty weights attached to their ankles. First, the REB therapist/coach needs to help the person remove their ankle weights (i.e. address their emotional disturbance) before discussing the best way to climb the hill (address the issue of development).

## Dissatisfaction before Development

Abraham Maslow (1968) is perhaps best known for his work on self-actualisation. The relevance of this concept for our present discussion is this. It is challenging for humans to focus on higher-order 'needs' when they are preoccupied with lower-order 'needs'. Thus, if a client is faced with a broad dissatisfying life experience, which cannot be compartmentalised, and also wants to explore theirwish to develop themself, then the REBT therapist/coach needs to help them with the former first before the latter.

## REBT with Emotional Problems

In this book, I have concentrated on REBT with clients who have emotional problems. Thus, when a client has an emotional problem, the REB therapist uses the ABC framework to assess both the problem and the potential REBT-based solution to the problem based on the client's problem-related goals. Then the therapist encourages the client to examine both the rigid/extreme attitudes that underpin the problem and the alternative flexible/non-extreme attitudes that could provide the solution to the problem. Once the client has committed themself to develop their flexible/non-extreme attitude, the therapist helps them embark on a process to strengthen their conviction in this attitude to help them reach their goals.

## REBT with Dissatisfaction Issues

If a client seeks help with a dissatisfaction-based problem, the therapist will help them differently. For example, the therapist may select a problem-solving framework such as the PRACTICE framework outlined by Palmer (2008) – see Table 7.1.

Suppose in the course of this work the client disturbs themself about some aspect of the situation. In that case, the therapist will revert to using REBT with emotional problems before returning to the dissatisfaction-based work.

## REBT to Promote Development

If a client seeks help to develop themself in one or more areas of their life, the REB therapist's interventions are indistinguishable from Rational Emotive Behavioural Coaching (REBC). Here, the therapist helps the person set development-based objectives informed by their strengths, values, and rational principles of living (Dryden, 2018a). Concerning the latter, the REB therapist uses the following principles to guide the discussion: self-interest, social interest, self-direction, self-acceptance, tolerance of others, short-term and long-term hedonism, commitment to creative, absorbing activities and pursuits, risk-taking and experimenting, discomfort tolerance and willpower, problem-solving, scientific thinking and flexibility (Bernard, 2018). Once a development-based objective has been set, the REB therapist helps the client construct an action plan to facilitate this objective's achievement. Suppose along the way, the client hits an emotionally-based obstacle to the achievement of their development-based objective. In that case, the therapist uses the

**Table 7.1** The PRACTICE Problem-Solving Framework (adapted from Palmer, 2008)

|  | Thinking steps | Examples of problem-solving thinking |
|---|---|---|
| P | **P**roblem identification | • What is the problem or issue that I need to focus on? |
| R | **R**ealistic, relevant goal development | • What are the goals or objectives that I can realistically work towards, ones that will make a real difference for me? |
| A | **A**lternative potential solutions generated | • What have I tried already that has not worked?<br>• Were there any elements of what I tried that were helpful on which I can build?<br>• What are the possible ways that I can solve the problem or reach my goal or objective? |
| C | **C**onsideration of potential solutions | • What do I think of each of the potential solutions (e.g. what are their consequences?; are they consistent with my values?; what other aspects of each possible solution do I have to consider? |
| T | **T**arget most feasible potential solution | • Having looked at each potential solution and its consequences which one is likely to be the most feasible one that I can select? |
| I | **I**mplementation of chosen potential solution | • How am I going to best implement the chosen potential solution? |
| C | **C**onsolidation of the chosen potential solution | • How am I going to ensure that I have given the chosen potential solution the best chance to see if it yields the results I want? |
| E | **E**valuation | • How successful was the potential solution? If so, it becomes the solution.<br>• If not, I need to try another potential solution until I find one that works |

ABC framework to help the client deal with this obstacle and return to pursuing this objective. For more information about Rational Emotive Behavioural Coaching see Dryden (2018a, 2018b).

While REBT has a preferred order in dealing with problems and issues as discussed above, it is important to reiterate that it values flexibility. Thus, if a client wants to deal with their problems in a different order and maintain this position even after their REB therapist has given their rationale for the disturbance-dissatisfaction-development order, their wishes should be accommodated to see what happens when the work follows their preferences.

•

\*

We have reached the end of this book, but before closing, I will provide some further reading suggestions for those wishing to learn more about REBT. I hope you have found this book of value. If you have any feedback, please email me at windy@windydryden.com

# Further Reading

For those seeking a comprehensive guide to the practice of REBT, I suggest:

- DiGiuseppe, R. A., Doyle, K. A., Dryden, W., and Backx, W. (2014). *A Practitioner's Guide to Rational Emotive Behavior Therapy.* 3<sup>rd</sup> edition. New York: Oxford University Press.

For those looking for a client REBT workbook that can be used in conjunction with therapy or by clients on their own, I suggest:

- Dryden, W. (2021). *Reason to Change: A Rational Emotive Behaviour Therapy (REBT) Workbook.* 2<sup>nd</sup> edition. Abingdon, Oxon: Routledge.

The following two linked edited texts are designed to provide state-of-the-art information on the REBT theory, practice and research:

- Bernard, M. E., and Dryden, W. (eds) (2019). *Advances in REBT: Theory, Practice, Research, Measurement, Prevention and Promotion.* Switzerland AG: Springer Nature.
- Dryden, W., and Bernard, M. E. (eds) (2019). *REBT with Diverse Client Problems and Populations.* Switzerland AG: Springer Nature.

There are numerous REBT self-help books on the market. Here is the one I usually recommend to my clients:

- Dryden, W. (2014). *Ten Steps to Positive Living.* 2<sup>nd</sup> edition. London: Sheldon Press.

109

# References

Beck, A. T. (1976). *Cognitive Therapy and the Emotional Disorders*. New York: International Universities Press.

Bernard, M. E. (2018). Rationality in coaching. In M. E. Bernard and David, O. (2018). *Coaching Reason, Emotion and Behavior Change: Rational-Emotive, Cognitive-Behavioral Practices* (pp. 51–66). New York: Springer.

Bordin, E. S. (1979). The generalizability of the psychoanalytic concept of the working alliance. *Psychotherapy: Theory, Research and Practice, 16(3)*, 252–60.

DiGiuseppe, R. A., Doyle, K. A., Dryden, W., and Backx, W. (2014). *A Practitioner's Guide to Rational Emotive Behavior Therapy*. 3rd edition. New York: Oxford University Press.

DiGiuseppe, R., Leaf, R., and Linscott, J. (1993). Thetherapeutic relationship in rational-emotive therapy: Some preliminary data. *Journal of Rational-Emotive and Cognitive-Behavior Therapy, 11*, 223–233.

Dryden, W. (1985). Challenging but not overwhelming: A compromise in negotiating homework assignments. *British Journal of Cognitive Psychotherapy, 3*(1), 77–80.

Dryden, W. (1998). Understanding persons in the context of their problems: A rational emotive behaviour therapy perspective. In M. Bruch and F. W. Bond (eds), *Beyond Diagnosis: Case Formulation Approaches in CBT* (pp. 43–64). Chichester: John Wiley & Sons.

Dryden, W. (2011). *Counselling in a Nutshell. 2$^{nd}$ Edition.* London: Sage.

Dryden, W. (2016). *Attitudes in Rational Emotive Behaviour Therapy: Components, Characteristics and Adversity-Related Consequences.* London: Rationality Publications.

Dryden, W. (2018a). *Rational Emotive Behavioural Coaching: Distinctive Features.* Abingdon, Oxon: Routledge.

Dryden, W. (2018b). *A Practical Guide to Rational Emotive Behavioural Coaching.* Abingdon, Oxon: Routledge.

Dryden, W. (2019). *Single-Session 'One-At-A-Time' Therapy: A Rational Emotive Behaviour Therapy Approach.* Abingdon, Oxon: Routledge.

Dryden, W. (2020). Awfulizing: Some conceptual and therapeutic considerations. *Journal of Rational-Emotive and Cognitive-Behavior Therapy, 38,* 295–305.

Dryden, W. (2021a). *The Working Alliance in Rational Emotive Behaviour Therapy: Principles and Practice.* Abingdon, Oxon: Routledge.

Dryden, W. (2021b). *Reason to Change: A Rational Emotive Behaviour Therapy Workbook.* 2$^{nd}$ Edition. Abingdon, Oxon: Routledge.

Dryden, W. (2021c). *Rational Emotive Behaviour Therapy,* 3$^{rd}$ Edition. Abingdon, Oxon: Routledge.

Ellis, A. (1957). Rational psychotherapy and individual psychology. *Journal of Individual Psychology, 13*(1), 38–44.

Ellis, A. (1959). Requisite conditions for basic personality change. *Journal of Consulting Psychology, 23,* 538–40.

Ellis, A. (1963). Toward a more precise definition of 'emotional' and 'intellectual' insight. *Psychological Reports, 13,* 125–6.

Ellis, A. (1985). Dilemmas in giving warmth or love to clients: An interview with Albert Ellis. In W. Dryden, *Therapists' Dilemmas* (pp. 5–16). London: Harper & Row.

Kuyken, W., Padesky, C. A., and Dudley, R. (2009). *Collaborative Case Conceptualization: Working Effectively with Clients in Cognitive-Behavioral Therapy.* Guilford Press.

Lazarus, A. A. (1993). Tailoring the therapeutic relationship, or being an authentic chameleon. *Psychotherapy: Theory, Research, Practice, Training, 30*(3), 404–7.

Mahrer, A. (ed.) (1967). *The Goals of Psychotherapy.* Englewood Cliffs, NJ: Prentice-Hall.

Maslow, A. (1968). *Toward a Psychology of Being.* New York: Van Nostrand Reinhold.

Palmer, S. (2008). The PRACTICE model of coaching: Towards a solution-focused approach. *Coaching Psychology International, 1*(1), 4–6.

Persons, J. B. (1989). *Cognitive Therapy in Practice: A Case Formulation Approach.* New York: W.W. Norton & Co.

Rogers, C. R. (1957). The necessary and sufficient conditions of therapeutic personality change. *Journal of Consulting Psychology, 21*, 95–103.

Woods, P. J. (1991). Orthodox RET taught effectively with graphics, feedback on irrational beliefs, a structured homework series, and models of disputation. In M. E. Bernard (ed.), *Using Rational-Emotive Therapy Effectively: A Practitioner's Guide* (pp. 69–109). New York: Plenum.

# Index

*Page numbers in bold refer to main principles; page numbers in italics refer to figures and tables.*

www.ingramcontent.com/pod-product-compliance
Lightning Source LLC
Chambersburg PA
CBHW050532280326
41933CB00011B/1559

* 9 7 8 1 9 1 0 3 0 1 9 1 3 *